THE NATIONAL ARCHIVES: IMAGES OF POWER AND MAJESTY

ROYAL SEALS

THE NATIONAL ARCHIVES: IMAGES OF POWER AND MAJESTY

ROYAL SEALS

PAUL DRYBURGH

PEN & SWORD HISTORY

AN IMPRINT OF PEN & SWORD BOOKS LTD.
YORKSHIRE – PHILADELPHIA

First published in Great Britain in 2020 by
Pen and Sword History
An imprint of
Pen & Sword Books Ltd
Yorkshire - Philadelphia

ISBN 978 1 52672 953 8

A CIP catalogue record for this book is available from the British Library.

The National Archives logo device is a trade mark of The National Archives and is used under licence. The National Archives logo © Crown Copyright 2018 © Crown Copyright images reproduced by permission of The National Archives, London England, 2018. The National Archives is the official archives and publisher for the UK Government, and for England and Wales. We work to bring together and secure the future of the public record, both digital and physical, for future generations. The National Archives is open to all, offering a range of activities and spaces to enjoy, as well as our reading rooms for research. Many of our most popular records are also available online.

Images of the seals prefixed with The National Archives reference DL are the property of Her Majesty the Queen in Right of Her Duchy of Lancaster and have been reproduced by kind permission of the Chancellor and Council of Her Majesty's Duchy of Lancaster.

Typeset in Minion Pro 11/14.5 by
SJmagic DESIGN SERVICES, India.

Printed and bound in India by Replika Press Pvt. Ltd.

Pen & Sword Books Ltd incorporates the Imprints of Pen & Sword Books Archaeology, Atlas, Aviation, Battleground, Discovery, Family History, History, Maritime, Military, Naval, Politics, Railways, Select, Transport, True Crime, Fiction, Frontline Books, Leo Cooper, Praetorian Press, Seaforth Publishing, Wharncliffe and White Owl.

For a complete list of Pen & Sword titles please contact

PEN & SWORD BOOKS LIMITED
47 Church Street, Barnsley, South Yorkshire, S70 2AS, England
E-mail: enquiries@pen-and-sword.co.uk
Website: www.pen-and-sword.co.uk

or

PEN AND SWORD BOOKS
1950 Lawrence Rd, Havertown, PA 19083, USA
E-mail: Uspen-and-sword@casematepublishers.com
Website: www.penandswordbooks.com

CONTENTS

ACKNOWLEDGEMENTS

It will be obvious to anyone who reads this book and knows the history of the collection of seals at The National Archives that my principal debt is to Dr Adrian Ailes. Adrian retired in 2016 from his role as Principal Records Specialist (Early Modern Records). In the two years between my appointment in 2014 and his departure, Adrian nurtured my interest in seals (which I will freely admit was not particularly strong) and guided me to a growing appreciation. I cannot do justice in this book to his expertise or to the loss researchers at TNA will feel at my taking over the seals brief from Adrian. However, I hope even a tiny fraction of his knowledge and enthusiasm is evident here.

Other colleagues past and present have helped immensely in bringing this book to fruition. Chief among them is conservation scientist Dr Elke Cwiertnia, with whom Adrian and I worked on the Wax Seals in Context project at TNA in 2014-16. Elke's knowledge and willingness to experiment brought new findings on the chemical and physical composition of seals, some of which is reflected here. The illustrations in chapter 4 are hers and are reproduced here by permission of the Collection Care Department at TNA. Amy Sampson, Preventive Conservator in the same department, has given me many opportunities to broaden my knowledge by involving me with her project to digitise our collection of seals moulds. The expertise and friendship of colleagues within the Medieval, Early Modern, Legal and Maps and Plans team has also provided a tremendous boon; rarely will one meet a more knowledgeable, engaged and engaging group of specialists in their field.

Ela Kaczmarska, Publishing Executive at TNA, has smoothed all of the internal processes involved in seeing this book to production, while both Alice Wright and Aileen Pringle of Pen & Sword have patiently, very patiently, steered me towards publication.

My debt is to you all.

Paul Dryburgh,
October 2020

INTRODUCTION

On most days – perhaps even several times a day – many of us will need to display and prove we are who we say we are in order to live our ordinary lives. More and more across the world, we identify ourselves and so validate and give force to our wishes in a virtual world where digital tools and methods are transforming the personal relationships and interactions which for centuries have governed our existence. The encoding and encryption of personal data in, for instance, chip and pin and Quick Response (QR) technology allows us to shop, bank and travel with greater freedom, while smart phones can now operate with fingerprint and facial recognition software to keep us in touch with loved ones, friends and the latest news instantly, and (hopefully) prevent others accessing our information. Email signatures and online password-protected accounts enable (in theory at least) secure communication, and business and legal transactions from the comfort of our workspace or armchair, and permit companies and government agencies to carry out their functions efficiently and effectively. However, the principle by which individuality and identity is embodied in something impersonal is not a modern invention. For many centuries, in a society where the written word is king in communication, we have employed two major means of proving our identity and showing our agreement to financial and legal acts, such as the acknowledgement and payment of debts and transfer of land or property. The signature – almost as individual as any fingerprint – has long conveyed our identity and assent literally writ large, but has done so only since about the fifteenth century; throughout the Middle Ages, even prior to the Norman Conquest, though to a decreasing extent from the eighteenth century, the primary medium through which individuals, communities and institutions authenticated and validated their identity and intentions was the seal.

Seals tell us so much about the status of their owner, give historical information around their imagery, and can help to date the document to which they are attached. Through this combination of text, image and material form, seals encrypt aspects of identity in a written record and those which an individual or group wish to reflect about themselves to the outside world. They are miniature marvels of their age and are fascinating glimpses into other worlds of art, thought, humour, trade, labour, majesty and power.

What is a seal?

The seal is simple but effective technology. The term can mean either a matrix (or die) cast from a hard substance, usually but not exclusively metal, into which an image or personal mark has been engraved, or, customarily, the impression, that same personal mark made by the matrix into a soft material like wax, shellac or clay. Both conveyed personal or corporate symbolism that helped identify the owner and displayed their status and office and, perhaps, something of their wit and personality. Matrices could come in many shapes and sizes, from a signet ring into which a Roman intaglio gemstone might be secured, to something that looks like a chess piece with a handle at the top (often to be placed on a chain and hung around the owner's neck) and the image engraved in the base, to a press. Some presses, like that at Canterbury Cathedral, are enormous screw mechanisms, others, like those for the medieval English royal great seals, are made up of two plates between which cakes of wax are sandwiched and then pressed together using lugs and lugholes.

The process of sealing has its origins deep in ancient history; the Assyrians, Babylonians and Egyptians all had cause to impress a visual message into clay or wax, often via a cylindrical device. Throughout history, seals have also been used to close (and so 'seal' shut) important objects, whether that be a letter from the monarch to an official or a chest full of written records or jewels and plate, in order to keep the contents safe and/or their meaning unchanged. But principally, the message and use of a seal relates to identity and authority.

The message a seal conveys is captured in an image – technically known as the 'device'. The image is usually accompanied by the legend, the inscribed text around the perimeter that confirms the identity of the seal owner, whether by name or in an allegorical or religious motto, and so helps authenticate the transaction to which it is attached. The list of potential images used as devices is large and habitually relates to status or occupation – the king and leading nobles, for example, often used their coat of arms as a marker of elite status to tie them into a long, powerful descent. They also tend to be depicted on horseback in full armour, which displays their fighting prowess, wealth and social standing, as well as their conformity to the latest fashions. Others – knights, gentlemen and women – often also use heraldic imagery; but this can diverge from simple coats of arms to animals (lions and eagles, to name but a few), mythical or Biblical beasts (the Agnus Dei – Lamb of God, complete with its flag – is very popular,

PRO 23/335A: Mould of the seal of Shaftesbury abbey (Dorset), taken from E 322/211, the abbey's deed of surrender (1539).

for instance, as the symbol of Christ), and flora (lilies, roses). Noble and gentle women also marked their status in their seals. They are often depicted standing inside an oval-shaped (or vesical) seal. Elite women can be shown wearing elaborate gowns and head-dresses and bearing a bird of prey (often a falcon) on their wrist to highlight their nobility, and perhaps a lily to show their purity. Some women can be seen carrying books, a sign of their learning. Others simply use heraldic imagery to tie themselves into their own parental or their husband's lineage. For institutions like monasteries or the mayor and bailiffs of a town, there might be a depiction of the building to which the seal related; some of these, for religious houses like Shaftesbury abbey in Dorset, are truly spectacular.

It is important to say, though, that as the Middle Ages progressed, access to sealing technology and the importance of seals in authenticating legal transactions widened the community of people who owned and used seals, right down to the upper levels of the peasantry in villages and manors across the country. Off-the-shelf designs could be purchased from vendors, often made from cheaper metals and with a huge range of devices from which to choose. Any design chosen from an almost countless assortment that included religious imagery – saintly or Biblical figures, for example – animals, birds and flowers could be used. Many people also borrowed the seal of a friend, the clerk writing the document or a legal official to express their will to a transaction, the documentary text of which they perhaps could not read and fully understand. After all, most land transactions were written in Latin well into the sixteenth century and even beyond. The physical act of applying a seal to a document before trusted witnesses could be as authoritative as the seal itself. This, of course, sometimes makes it impossible to link the identity of the owner of a matrix from which an impression would be made to the people named in a particular document.

By the fifteenth century, the growing use of the signature as the personal mark and also this weakening of the personal connection between seal owner and transaction led to a decline in the use of seals. Nonetheless, the signature and seal were often combined on documents for another couple of centuries, even as the signature gradually took over from the seal in terms of authentication. As western nations gained empires overseas, so the use of seals in business spread around the world; but sealing never regained its medieval height. Still, the seal retained legal force as the main authenticator into the modern age, and many seals were probably borrowed from the lawyer or legal practitioner processing the business, as their use was imperative even into the twentieth century, especially in property and land transactions. Modern companies and government departments still retain official seals. Schemes such as the Charter Mark, introduced by the Conservative government in the 1990s, for instance, adapted medieval ideas around the creation and projection of self-imagery in law to authenticate and award excellent practice in public service into the twenty-first century.

How were documents sealed?
In practical terms, documents could be sealed in one of several ways. On more formal grants and transactions during the Middle Ages and Renaissance period, the sealing wax often hung from the bottom of the parchment upon which the text was written. Parchment is animal skin, often taken from sheep or goats, but in

more important documents vellum, or calfskin – the very finest comes from the skins of stillborn animals – was used. Parchment and vellum are incredibly robust and could be produced relatively cheaply as a by-product of animal husbandry. A fold was made upwards in the parchment to make what is called the plica. A slit or holes were then cut and, depending on the formality of the transaction, (coloured) silken or hemp laces or a separate strip of parchment were threaded through the slit or holes. The seal would be attached to the pendent tag. This permitted seals with imagery on both sides to be viewed easily. Alternatively, government orders, which were often written to officials on narrow pieces of parchment, or documents bearing the seals of many parties might have the seal(s) attached to a tongue or tongues cut as thin strips from the bottom edge of the document. Finally, seals could be applied to documents directly to their face, known in French as *en placard*. This was achieved by dropping melted wax onto the surface and pressing the matrix into the hot substance. Speed and skilful wax preparation ensured a decent and lasting impression. Each method had legal force but was adapted to the size, nature and legal context of the document.

Seals at The National Archives

Matrices often survive as archaeological discoveries or archival antiquities in national and local museums and archaeological collections, perhaps most notably in the British Museum. The majority of surviving seals though are those hundreds of thousands of impressions in wax from the British Isles and overseas to be found in archives and libraries across the United Kingdom. The National Archives (TNA) holds the UK's greatest collection of wax seal impressions (but no matrices), comprising over 250,000 seals dating from the eleventh to the twentieth century. The collection is of international importance. TNA is the archive of royal government back to *Domesday Book* in the eleventh century – the first 'public record', which are those documents created by or for government in pursuing its business according to law. The collection includes royal, governmental and colonial seals but also examples of ecclesiastical, monastic, topographical and personal seals.

The aim of this book is to guide you through this internationally important collection and give you an up-close look at some of the finest examples of medieval and modern craftsmanship and art anywhere in the UK today. The book is divided into four chapters, each taking a different type of seal owner as its theme: royal seals (essentially the Great Seal but including other princely seals); personal seals (armorial and non-armorial, men and women); and ecclesiastical seals (of individuals and institutions). The final chapter looks at the materials used in creating seal impressions and some of the science behind it. I hope you find it enjoyable and informative.

CHAPTER 1

ROYAL SEALS

Seals are some of the most ornate and beautiful depictions of the power and majesty of monarchy to survive from any age. They truly represent the formal status and authority of the crown and, at certain moments, the personal will of the sovereign. Seals therefore have a long history in the government of this country. Anglo-Saxon kings had used seals to express their authority. Coenwulf, king of Mercia (796-821), for example, had a seal. But in England the adoption by William the Conqueror (1066-1087) of the practice of his immediate predecessor Edward the Confessor (1042-1066) cemented the process and ritual of sealing in English royal administrative and political culture to the present day.

Both the Confessor and the Conqueror used seals as a form of authenticating their wishes officially, most often when attached to royal charters and writs, those tiny strips of parchment on which royal commands were issued, but the sign manual (often a simple cross) was also used. Both Edward and William used a round seal depicting the king seated on his throne holding the regalia of kingship – the orb and sceptre – representing Christian authority and the promise to uphold law and rule justly. Their successors developed increasingly more elaborate imagery as we will see throughout this chapter. Principally, the development under the Confessor and the Conqueror of an image on the back of the seal with the monarch on horseback came more clearly to represent the martial prowess and status of the monarch. This equestrian imagery persisted for many centuries, the main exceptions being Queen Anne (1702-1714), who depicted herself as the mythical Britannia, and George V (1910-1935), who wears his naval uniform and stands proudly on the prow of his warship.

However, as the areas under English rule changed over time, so the great seals changed to reflect that. Edward III (1327-1377), for example, added the fleurs-de-lys of France to the three lions of England on his coat of arms on the majesty side of his great seal after 1340 to reinforce his hereditary claim to be king of France and England.

T 40/4: Portrait of Queen Anne, 1702.

DL 10/324: Great seal of Edward III, obverse, 1361.

Elizabeth I (1558-1603) added the Irish harp to her second great seal from 1586 to demonstrate her claim to the kingdom of Ireland. It is worth noting at this point that kings of Scotland and princes of Wales (before 1301 – the first 'English' prince) also used the great seal to authenticate their acts.

In order to create these double-sided great seals, the metal matrix consisted of two plates – the obverse (or front) and the reverse (or back) – the internal faces of which were engraved with an image and legend.

DL 27/37: Seal of William the Lion, king of Scotland, obverse, 1165-74.

SC 13/H22: Seal of Alexander III, king of Scotland, obverse, 1249-86.

SC 13/H22: Seal of Alexander III, king of Scotland, reverse, 1249-86.

Two cakes of softened wax would then be sandwiched between the plates which were then squeezed together by the use of two to four lugs on one plate and the same number of pins on the other which were then screwed into place or rolled under pressure, to make as crisp an impression as possible. The cords or tag were placed between the cakes to make a pendent seal that would hang from a royal grant or award. Oil and/or chalk could then be used to ease the wax from the matrix before it was attached to the document. At this elite level, seal matrices were made by goldsmiths, some of the most skilled craftsmen of their day: the boy king Henry III (1216-1272) had his new matrix engraved by the goldsmith Walter de Ripa, for example, in 1218. In Henry's case, this symbolically and physically demonstrated the kingdom's break from the tyranny of his unpopular father, John (1199-1216).

As it represented the highest authority in the land, the royal great seal had a special status. It was held safely by the chancellor, the official who presided over the king's writing office and who in the twelfth and thirteenth centuries often remained with the king as he journeyed around his dominions or engaged in warfare and diplomacy. This meant the great seal and its derivatives could be used with relative speed to put the king's wishes into effect. It also meant that forgery of the great seal would theoretically be punishable by death, at least until the Forgery Act of 1913. The great seal matrix would be transferred between chancellors and would be the subject of intimate rituals, sometimes in the royal chamber, when the monarch either instituted new officials or left the country on business, thereby delegating power to a lieutenant or regent. The inherently personal and legal nature of the great seal – its attachment to an individual king or queen and its primary use in authenticating legal or financial business – meant that it was usual for the seal matrix of the late monarch to be ceremonially broken before witnesses, or reconfigured in some way upon their death and the accession of a new sovereign. Where a seal matrix had become worn out through use or where a political or diplomatic transformation had occurred in the country, perhaps through victory in warfare or marriage of the sovereign, a new seal could be commissioned by a living monarch to reflect these changes iconographically. The first great seal of Henry III was apparently broken up and the pieces shared out between 'poor people belonging to a certain religious house'. Henry's grandson, Edward II (1307-1327), had two small castles cut into his father's final matrix as a mark of distinction and to denote his Spanish

T 40/1C: Portrait of King William III (Duke William of Orange), 1684.

heritage from his mother, Eleanor of Castile. Likewise, preventing a rival or potential successor from instituting a legitimate royal authority could, it was believed in some cases, be achieved by ensuring they could not access the great seal. In an act of supreme but futile political defiance the Catholic king James II (1685-1688) threw his matrix into the River Thames in December 1688 while fleeing London before William of Orange, only for a local fisherman to recover it for the new royal couple. Consequently, his abdication and the new reign of William III (1688-1702) and his wife Mary II (1688-1694) date to this event.

In theory, then, throughout many centuries, all major acts of state had to be authenticated with the great seal. For most people, if they saw it at all, the seal on a royal document could be their main, perhaps only, personal interaction with and reception of monarchy apart from the coinage. The act of holding or viewing a royal document complete with impressive, glinting seal would convey in ways the formal text could never do the majesty of the owner and the power of the crown. If size matters, then it is important to note that the royal great seals increased in both diameter and thickness, if only gradually, over the centuries. In the twelfth century, Henry I's seals measured around 8-9cm in diameter while his successors' grew around 0.2cm per reign to reach around 10cm by the mid fourteenth century. By the twentieth century, the great seal had grown to around 15cm. Similarly, in terms of the thickness of the impression, and the relief of the figures rising from the wax, these grew gradually from, respectively, c. 1-1.3cm (figures) and 0.5-0.75cm (edges) in the twelfth century to c. 2cm (figures) and 0.5cm (edges) during the reign of Edward I (1272-1307). This, of course, meant the impression itself had become increasingly defined, elaborate and crisp and the visual power of monarchy thereby radically redefined. Naturally, this introduced greater expense on materials and skilled craftsmen for making both the matrix and the impression. The use of new materials – metals, shellacs and plastics – and new artistic techniques and modes of expressing the image of majesty, especially in portraiture, has changed the modern great seal in physical make-up and dimension but not necessarily in its artistic value.

As the archive of English – and later British – royal government, The National Archives holds hundreds of examples of royal great seals. Unfortunately, we hold no surviving seal which dates earlier than the reign of William II (1087-1100), and this survives only in two fragments [DL 10/1; E 326/12623]. However, our collection is continuous thereafter and includes multiple examples of the great seal of each subsequent sovereign (in various states of repair and fineness) as well as the Commonwealth of England during the Interregnum in the seventeenth century.

The two great seals of William the Conqueror survive in a handful of examples. His is the first in England to employ imagery on the obverse (of the warrior mounted on horseback charging to the right, wearing a chainmail tunic and conical helmet and holding a lance in the right hand with a banner flying from it, and a kite-shaped Norman shield in his left hand) and reverse (of the king seated in majesty wearing a crown of three points while holding a sword in the right hand and an orb mounted with a cross in the left). On the obverse is the Latin legend HOC NORMANNORVM WILLELMVM NOSCE PATRONVM SI ('Recognise by this that William is the protector of the Normans or') and on the reverse it continues HOC ANGLIS REGEM SIGNO FATEARIS EVNDEM ('by this sign acknowledge that the same is king to the English'). The beauty of this seal is that it enabled William to use one matrix in both his kingdom of England and his dukedom of Normandy and convey his power and majesty in both contexts. The imagery and language are very carefully and tellingly chosen. His son William II ('Rufus') employs very similar imagery in his two great seals bar a five-pointed crown secured to the king's head by a chin-strap, and the insertion of stars on either side of the enthroned monarch – this image of majesty transferred to the obverse where it permanently stayed. However, having not succeeded his father as duke of Normandy, Rufus altered the legend on his great seal to read WILLELMVS DEI GR[ATI]A REX ANGLORV[M] ('William, by the grace of God, king of the English'). This use of God's grace emphasised the sacred authority of William's crown (similarly, the image of the king holding an orb with a cross on top highlights his Christian authority in the world), and it remains in the royal style to this day – though, of course, the precise nature of grace was disputed at certain moments.

We are now going to look at the seals of a selection of monarchs in a little more detail and examine the context behind the creation of new imagery in the process.

HENRY I (1100-1135)
During his long reign, Henry I, youngest son of the Conqueror, appears to have used at least three, perhaps four different great seal matrices, which reflects the changes in his title and his fluctuating political and military fortunes. Henry's reign also witnessed an explosion in the production and use of records as the culture of writing began to spread and gain greater effective legal force.

The first (often known as the second) great seal is similar in imagery to those of his father and brother, with the enthroned, crowned king bearing sword and orb on the obverse and riding on horseback in a heavy mail-shirt (the hauberk) with lance and shield in hand on the reverse. This seal was used until around 1106/7 when it was replaced by the second (known as the third).

E 42/317: Charter of King Henry granting that Holy Trinity Priory, London, shall be free from subjection to all churches, and granting them £25 yearly in rents at Exeter (1107 x 1123), natural wax with varnish applied. Second/Third Great Seal of Henry I, obverse.

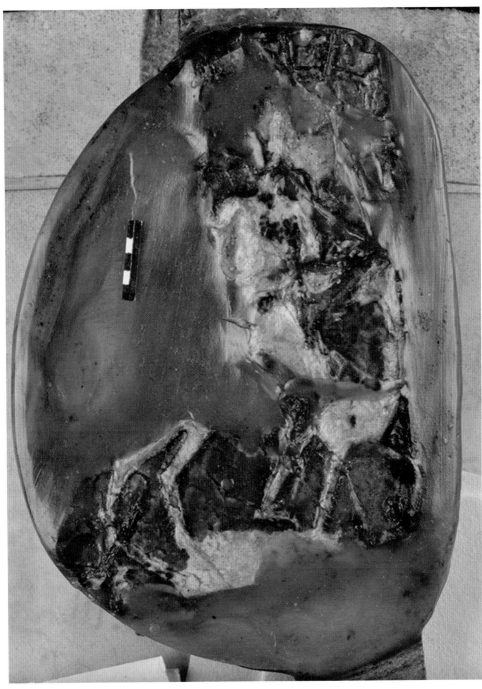

E 42/317: Charter of King Henry granting that Holy Trinity Priory, London, shall be free from subjection to all churches, and granting them £25 yearly in rents at Exeter (1107 x 1123), natural wax with varnish applied. Second/Third Great Seal of Henry I, reverse.

Though similar, a major stylistic difference is the appearance of a dove atop the cross on the orb, a symbol of both peace and the Holy Spirit.

This may reflect Henry's victory over his older brother Robert duke of Normandy at Tinchebrai in Normandy on 28 September 1106. Part of Henry's campaign to extend and cement his authority over the Anglo-Norman realm and its nobility,

SC 13/H88, third/fourth great seal, 1121x1123-1135, natural wax, obverse.

the battle resulted in his brother's capture and imprisonment for the rest of his life to 1134 and Henry's installation as *de facto* duke of Normandy. This enabled him to establish relative peace, particularly in England. This new seal, however, does not reflect the change in status: the legend on both sides reads HENRICVS DEI GRACIA REX ANGLORVM ('Henry, by the grace of God, king of the English').

SC 13/H88, third/fourth great seal, 1121x1123-1135, natural wax, reverse.

Henry's visual assertion of his claim to the duchy of Normandy comes no sooner than around fifteen years later (the precise date of the change is unclear) after he had a third (known as fourth) great seal cut. The change came in the aftermath of the so-called 'White Ship' disaster of 25 November 1120 when Henry's son and heir William Ætheling drowned as the king's ship carrying William and dozens of his senior noblemen sank as it left Barfleur for England. The mourning king, deprived of the sole male heir of his body, to whom the barons of Normandy and England had done homage, added HENRICVS DEI GRATIA DUX NORMANNORVM ('Henry, by the grace of God, duke of the Normans') to the reverse side of his great seal. Two eight-pointed stars are placed either side of the king on the obverse while on the reverse the horse is now more muscular and there is more definition on the mail-shirt and Henry's sword, which now pierces the legend. Overall, the quality of the craftsmanship on the matrix is much higher than earlier examples.

STEPHEN (1135-1154)

Henry's successor, his nephew Stephen of Blois, count of Boulogne, keenly tied himself to his uncle's visual style in the two great seals produced during his turbulent reign, as you can see in his first great seal, in use from 1135 to around 1141.

However, when Stephen was captured in battle at Lincoln in February 1141 by forces loyal to his competitor for the throne, the Empress Matilda, daughter of Henry I, his matrix was either lost or seized. Upon his negotiated release after nine months in captivity and restoration to his throne, Stephen therefore had to commission a new matrix. The result was a larger great seal: the enthroned image of Stephen remained similar, though the orb is much smaller and the dove on top much larger, more like a crow! On the reverse, the horse is less well defined and Stephen's sword less grooved. A banner streams from his lance on which a cross pattée (a Christian cross whose arms are narrow close to the centre and then flare out towards the edge) is shown, symbolically displaying what he hoped would be the sacred support for his cause.

The battle for the crown was not just fought in the field, though. Matilda had to win hearts and minds and impress her authority upon England. Documents issued in her name bear a single-sided seal displaying the sacred power of royalty. Matilda sits on a throne wearing a crown of three points with her feet resting on a footstool; she wears a long robe to the ankles with

DL 10/12, Great Seal of King Stephen, 1135x1141, obverse.

DL 10/12, Great Seal of King Stephen, 1135x1141, reverse.

wide sleeves; in her right hand she holds a long sceptre with a fleur-de-lys on top but, unlike her rival and his predecessors, she does not hold an orb in her left hand. While married to her second husband, Geoffrey of Anjou, Matilda used her title as 'Queen of the Romans' on the legend of her seal, a reference to her first marriage, in 1114, to Heinrich V, Holy Roman Emperor, king of the Germans: S[IGILLVM] MATHILDIS DEI GRATIA ROMANORVM REGINA ('Seal of Matilda, by God's grace queen of the Romans'). This both conveyed a sense of her position in European royalty but also perhaps the practical difficulties she faced in asserting herself in England, where she did not have sufficient time or security in power to commission a great seal. Nevertheless, Matilda's beautiful great seal is the first depiction of female authority among English royal seals.

DL 10/16, Great Seal of Empress Matilda, 1142.

HENRY II (1154-1189)

The spoils of the struggle for power in England ultimately fell to Matilda, of course, when her son Henry came to the throne following Stephen's death in 1154 in a settlement negotiated before the late king's death. Henry II continued to use the essential iconography developed by his predecessors on his seal: on the obverse of his first great seal, in use from 1155, the enthroned king wears a three-pointed crown and carries a sword in his right hand and an orb in his left with the dove perched on top, and his legend reads 'Henry, by grace of God king of the English'; on the reverse, the king on horseback wears a conical helmet with nasal protection, brandishes a sword and bears a kite-shaped shield where the viewer can see the inside (not the outside with any heraldic design). The major difference comes in Henry's legend on the reverse: HENRICVS DUX NORMANNORVM ET AQUITANOR[VM] ET COM[ES] ANDEGAVOR[VM] ('Henry, duke of the Normans and Aquitainians and count of the Angevins'). This refers to Henry's inheritance of Normandy from his mother and Anjou from his father but also his right to Aquitaine, the duchy brought to Henry by his marriage in 1152 to Eleanor of Aquitaine almost immediately following her divorce from the French king Louis VII. These details changed little over the two other seals Henry used during his long reign.

Henry bequeathed much to his four legitimate sons – Henry (b. 1155), Richard (b. 1157), Geoffrey (b. 1158) and John (b. 1167) – not least the imagery to be used on the seals of those who followed him as king. This was despite an incredibly turbulent reign in which the eldest Henry (hence known as 'the Young King') was crowned as king during his father's lifetime, reigning from 1170, sharing royal business and leading rebellions against his father until his death in 1183. His siblings all rebelled against their father too. But Henry II's territorial ambitions and the rivalries his reign generated impacted on the dominions of the English crown, which encouraged some significant changes in the royal style of the great seals. Similarly, the increase in business dealt with by the king's chancery – his writing office – and exchequer – his financial office – as Henry innovated in his use of the law and as royal authority had to be imposed over dominions from the Scottish borders to the Pyrenees, meant that within a century of the great seal's effective introduction in England, it was no longer the only seal used to authorise all government business. The great manual of practice in the exchequer at this time, the *Dialogue of the Exchequer*, describes financial orders being written and sealed without the great seal being present. Certainly by the reign of Richard I, a separate, smaller Exchequer seal had been developed. This featured the three lions of England, familiar to us all, the first application of heraldry to a royal seal.

E 42/527, confirmation to the canons of Holy Trinity, London, of a grant of £25 a year, by weight, out of the rents of the city of Exeter for the souls of his grandparents, King Henry and Queen Matilda: second Great Seal of Henry II, obverse.

E 42/527, confirmation to the canons of Holy Trinity, London, of a grant of £25 a year, by weight, out of the rents of the city of Exeter for the souls of his grandparents, King Henry and Queen Matilda: second Great Seal of Henry II, reverse.

RICHARD I (1189-1199)

The first great seal of Richard I, in use until c. 1197, is an adaptation of his father's. The enthroned king wears a crown of three points on which are fleurs-de-lys. A grooved sword is held in the right hand while the left holds an orb which this time is not topped by a dove but a branch with four stems, the middle of which ends in a cross pattée. On either side of the king's head is a crescent and a six-pointed star. Sprays of flowers populate the

DL 10/47 Confirmation of the agreement between Beatrice de Say and Maud de Say on the division of the Say inheritance (originally dated 1185), 1198, second Great Seal, obverse.

DL 10/47 Confirmation of the agreement between Beatrice de Say and Maud de Say on the division of the Say inheritance (originally dated 1185), 1198, second Great Seal, reverse.

background on either side of the throne. Richard's style remains 'Richard, by the grace of God king of the English'. On the reverse, Richard wears conical helmet and mail-shirt while brandishing a sword. The shield now appears to reflect the heraldry appearing on his exchequer seal, with lions depicted on it. His horse appears to be galloping at a greater pace. The legend reads 'Richard, duke of the Normans and Aquitainians and count of the Angevins'.

In around 1197, Richard commissioned a new great seal. Part of his motivation was his need to rebuild the financial resources at his disposal after his crusade, which had ended with the king being ransomed out of captivity, and periodic war against Philip Augustus, king of France. The changes in Richard's imagery were subtle, with a single crescent appearing to the king's right and a single star to his left on the obverse, and a much clearer engraving of the three lions on his shield. Richard's helmet has a fanned-out crest on top with a lion on it, much more the epitome of the emerging cult of chivalry and military display. Lions traditionally symbolised royalty, nobility, courage, strength and valour, the apex of the animal kingdom, an apt symbol for the lion-hearted king.

JOHN (1199-1216)

Little of that description has traditionally been applied to Richard's youngest brother and successor, John, and it was under John that the royal style changed irredeemably. On ascending the throne, John adopted much of Richard's iconography but with minor adjustments. On the obverse, the star, crescent and flowers disappeared, and the legend was adjusted to reflect John's title of 'lord of Ireland'. Henry II had granted his son not only the county of Mortain in France but lordship (possibly even kingship) of Ireland, which Henry had at least partly subjected to his authority by a military intervention in 1172 and a series of treaties with Irish and English lords thereafter. In 1185, Henry sent John to Ireland to exercise personal lordship. While John's lordship in Ireland would not simply be asserted by military force but also by the more subtle arts of diplomacy, settlement and cultural change, success in the art of war was imperative in consolidating English control over Ireland. His superb seal as lord of Ireland displays John in full battle array surrounded by the legend 'Seal of John, son of the king of England, lord of Ireland', thereby capturing the spirit and practicalities of his new-found status.

C 109/86/4 Seal of John count of Mortain, lord of Ireland, c. 1185.

When, fourteen years later, John became king, his royal title reflected this change in the possessions of the English king: IOHANNES DEI GRATIA REX ANGLIE DOMINVS HIBERNIE ('John, by grace of God king of England, lord of Ireland'). Note the change in style from 'king of the English' to 'king of England'. On the reverse he retained 'John, duke of Normandy and Aquitaine and count of Anjou'. Interestingly, the style of some of the lettering changes from the angular Roman style to the more rounded Gothic, reflecting broader changes in art and architecture in the twelfth century.

DL 10/56 Grant to William Longespée, earl of Salisbury, of fairs at Long Sutton (Lincolnshire), and Middleton Stoney (Oxfordshire), 1202, Great Seal of King John, obverse.

DL 10/56 Grant to William Longespée, earl of Salisbury, of fairs at Long Sutton (Lincolnshire), and Middleton Stoney (Oxfordshire), 1202, Great Seal of King John, reverse.

HENRY III (1216-1272)

In 1204, John lost his duchy of Normandy and other continental possessions to the French, which wrought great changes in landholding among the aristocratic community subject to the English king. John's efforts to regain these lost lands culminated in his humiliating defeat at Bouvines in 1214. Throughout his reign, his increasingly arbitrary and tyrannical approach to kingship combined with the development of record making and record keeping, enabling the crown to keep better track of grants, rights and debts and impose new pressures on many sections of society. Civil war broke out and John was ultimately forced to grant numerous concessions in Magna Carta of June 1215. When John died at Newark in October 1216, the fate of England hung in the balance: his baronial opponents had rallied to Louis, son of the French king, and Louis's invasion force had to be tackled in the name of John's nine-year-old son, Henry, by the regent William Marshal and his aides. Only victories in battles on land at Lincoln in May 1217 and at sea off Sandwich shortly thereafter settled the conflict and secured the crown of the young Henry. Once the chaos had abated and attempts were made to return government to something resembling normality, a royal council met in November 1218, presided over by Stephen Langton, archbishop of Canterbury, the architect of Magna Carta. There, a new great seal was commissioned for Henry. His first seal great seal is a masterpiece of medieval craftsmanship which, in portraying Henry in adult majesty, disguised his youth and incapacity to rule in his own right. Henry sits on a throne without a back. At his feet are two small lions. In his right hand is a sword and in his left an orb from which foliage rises and on top of which sits a cross. On the reverse, a beautifully engraved, energetic horse carries Henry in full armour, sword in one hand, an heraldic shield in the other. Henry's helmet is now visored shut and is topped by his crown in a display of martial majesty. The legends are deeply political; the obverse has 'Henry, by the grace of God king of England, lord of Ireland' but the reverse still announces Henry's claim to the continental dominions – Normandy and Anjou – lost by his father but which he would spend decades trying to recover, 'Henry, duke of Normandy and Aquitaine, count of Anjou'.

Henry's first seal remained in use for forty years until further political, military and diplomatic developments forced a change. In 1259, Henry ordered the cutting of a second great seal. A year earlier, a political revolution had brought the king to rely on a council and baronial government led by his brother-in-law Simon de Montfort, earl of Leicester. By the Treaty of Paris of December 1259, Henry formally acknowledged that his campaigns to win

E 42/315 The King to Stanley Abbey: Grant of the moor of Alfletemore in exchange for a surrender of land and the right to take wood in Chippenham Forest (Wiltshire), 1227, first Great Seal of Henry III, obverse.

E 42/315 The King to Stanley Abbey: Grant of the moor of Alfletemore in exchange for a surrender of land and the right to take wood in Chippenham Forest (Wiltshire), 1227, first Great Seal of Henry III, reverse.

back his continental inheritance were forlorn, and he renounced to Louis IX, king of France, all claim to the duchy of Normandy and the provinces of Anjou, Maine, Poitou and Touraine. He also swore to perform homage for Aquitaine in southwestern France. Henry's new seal reflected this reality. The crowned Henry holds a sceptre in his right hand which is topped with a dove. While this reflects his role as a lawgiver, it also, of course, hints at his failure as a warrior king. His throne has a back now which is more richly ornamented than those of his predecessors. As well as the lions at his feet,

E 23/1/1 - Signet seal of Richard II attached to his will, April 1399, obverse.

two lions also stand rampant on either side of the foot of the throne. It is in the legends, though, that the change is most evident. On both sides Henry is described thus: 'Henry, by grace of God king of England, lord of Ireland, duke of Aquitaine'. Claims to Normandy and Anjou are no more. This was ritualistically and ceremonially demonstrated when, on 18 October 1260, Henry's first great seal was broken in his presence in the royal chamber at Westminster; the fragments were distributed among the poor brethren of certain religious houses.

E 23/1/1 - Signet seal of Richard II attached to his will, April 1399, reverse.

In the intervening period between his accession and the Treaty of Paris, the growth and sophistication of royal bureaucracy created a longer documentary trail that required new approaches to demonstrating the king's will. After a failed campaign to reassert English authority across the Channel in 1230, the now adult King Henry began to use a much smaller seal to send instructions to his chancellor to put his decisions into written effect. This became known as the privy seal. From this point, English kings made use of a privy seal as part of the machinery of government. As more and more business went 'out of court', they developed a succession of other seals, each closer to the person of the king, to try and get round a system that creaked under the weight of work. On the previous page is an example of the signet (or secret) seal of Henry's great-great-great grandson, Richard II (1377-1399), which was borne on a finger ring and was used to give more immediate effect to the king's wishes.

EDWARD I (1272-1307)

Henry's long reign, the longest in the Middle Ages, witnessed not only the failure to recover the crown's continental lands, it also saw a low point in the history of monarchy with the Montfortian revolution restraining Henry's power as king. Only with victory in battle at Evesham in August 1265 did Henry restore personal rule. Much of his recovery was down to his son, the Lord Edward, who eventually came to the throne as Edward I in November 1272 while on crusade in the Holy Land. Edward is one of England's most successful medieval kings, bringing English lordship to much of Wales and asserting sovereignty, if only for a short period, over Scotland. Political developments in his reign are also mirrored in sealing practices.

Edward used one great seal throughout his reign. Essentially, it mirrored that of his father's first seal, particularly in the fineness of its engraving. The major addition Edward made was an elaborate heraldic caparison for his warhorse, displaying the three lions as on his shield. But Edward not only adopted a privy seal like his father he also continued the use of what were known as 'deputed' seals for the English administrations in Ireland, in use no later than 1232, and Gascony, from the 1250s. These were smaller than the great seal in England but bore the same imagery, in order to impress the same royal majesty upon communities far distant from the centre of English royal power but which possessed the same bonds of loyalty and service. Over time, the majesty image on these deputed seals was replaced by the single shield of the royal arms of three lions *passant guardant* (lions walking to the left in a stalking pose, their heads turned to the viewer, with their tails raised above their backs). This visual symbolism played a role in the creation of English national identity and its association with monarchy; it is, of course, widely used today, most famously perhaps as the badge of the England football teams. When, however, Edward asserted his military and administrative authority in Scotland following the rebellion of the community of that kingdom to his overlordship in 1296, and the overthrow of King John Balliol, the English king commissioned a deputed seal for Scotland that replaced the equestrian image with the three lions of England.

Above left: E 39/29 letters patent of John de Balliol, 1292, with the seal of William Fraser, bishop of St Andrews, obverse.

Above right: E 39/29 letters patent of John de Balliol, 1292, with the seal of William Fraser, bishop of St Andrews, reverse.

This negated the authority of an independent Scottish king and demonstrated in wax the serious change in the balance of power in Anglo-Scots relations from equality to subjection. By 1304, Edward I had moved to establish a chancery and exchequer at Berwick after the submission of many of the elite community of Scotland in response to a winter campaign and an English army of occupation.

Ultimately, this proved to be as short-lived an experiment as English control of Scotland, which was challenged upon Robert Bruce's seizure of the Scottish throne in 1306 and Edward I's death in July 1307, and which did not long survive the succession of Edward's much less militarily successful son, Edward II (1307-1327).

EDWARD III (1327-1377)

Edward II's reign ended early in 1327 when the king was deposed for a litany of personal and political failings. An invasion force spearheaded by Edward's queen, Isabella, and their son, Edward of Windsor, had swept the king from power within only three months after landing in Suffolk from Holland. This was the first time a ruling monarch had been deposed by his people and may, rather more gruesomely, have ended in Edward's murder in captivity some months later. During that period, letters and orders had been issued in the name of the queen and her son but the great seal of the realm remained with the king. Once captive, Edward's seal fell into the hands of the new regime. With the pressure of time and the need to crown the boy king quickly and overturn some of the worst excesses of the previous reign, pardoning many people and restoring them to lands and properties seized from them, the new king, now Edward III, initially used his father's seal. This came complete with the two castles cut either side of the majesty portrait – believed to represent Edward II's Spanish heritage from his mother Eleanor of Castile – but with the addition of two fleurs-de-lys, to represent Edward's mother Isabella, daughter of Philip IV, late king of France.

Once Edward's reign had stabilised under the direction of his mother and her probable lover Roger Mortimer, soon to be first earl of March, this matrix was ceremonially broken at Nottingham in the presence of the young king in October 1327. It was replaced by a matrix on the obverse of which Edward sits on an elaborate throne with four pinnacles and niches behind his legs, the king holding a sceptre and orb topped with a cross. The castles of his father's seal have been removed but the fleurs-de-lys remain. On the reverse, Edward, who saw his first campaign as king in summer 1327 while approaching his fifteenth birthday, is dressed in full military array with a conical, visored helmet, sword, heraldic surcoat and shield and sat astride a dashing warhorse whose flashing

DL 10/281, Letters patent granting to John de Willington, Ralph, his son, and
Eleanor, his wife, Carreg Cennan castle, the commote of Iscennen (Carmarthenshire),
and the reversion of Broad Town, Orcheston St. George, and Elston (Wiltshire), 1337,
second Great Seal of Edward III, obverse.

DL 10/281, Letters patent granting to John de Willington, Ralph, his son, and Eleanor, his wife, Carreg Cennan castle, the commote of Iscennen (Carmarthenshire), and the reversion of Broad Town, Orcheston St. George, and Elston (Wiltshire), 1337, second Great Seal of Edward III, reverse.

tail is visible for the first time. This would prove an apt image for the king who would bring fire and sword to swathes of northern France in the early stages of the Hundred Years War from 1337.

This second great seal witnessed the transition of Edward to personal rule after his coup at Nottingham Castle in October 1330 toppled Roger Mortimer, who, with the queen, had ruled in his stead for four years, and the beginning of the Hundred Years' War. Indeed, dynastic and international politics fused with Edward's ambitions to change the iconography on his seals and those of his successors over several decades and, even, centuries.

In February 1340, Edward returned to England from a first continental campaign where he laid claim to the throne of France. A new temporary seal was cast to reflect this monumental change in his status. The king himself sits in majesty with a sceptre in his right hand topped with a fleur-de-lys and a cross-topped orb in his left. The throne is significantly more ornamental but the major change is the appearance of shields of arms on either side. These bear the quartered arms of France and England, with the fleurs-de-lys of France in the top-left and bottom-right quarters and the three lions of England in the top-right and bottom-left quarters, the heraldic expression of French superiority over England. These same arms also appear on the king's shield and horse saddlecloth and head-dress (or caparison) on the reverse. On both sides the legend also reflects this change: EDWARDVS DEI GRACIA REX FRANCIE ET ANGLIE D[OMI]N[V]S HYBERNIE ET DVX AQUITANIE ('Edward, by the grace of God king of France and England, lord of Ireland and duke of Aquitaine').

Over the next twenty years, Edward shuttled between England and France as his military campaigning brought totemic victories at Crécy (1346), after which the king besieged and captured Calais, and Poitiers (1356), where he seized and imprisoned the French king Jean II in 1356. Edward governed with two separate great seals, one for those periods of presence in England and one for those periods of absence abroad. In terms of quality, these seals are increasingly elaborate examples of the skills of the medieval goldsmith and largely show minor developments in the key stylistic features, particularly the carving of the throne. Perhaps the finest fourteenth-century example, though, is the seal Edward commissioned to mark the end of nearly twenty-five years of conflict. On 24 October 1360, England and France agreed a peace treaty at Brétigny near Chartres. Edward III won a series of territorial concessions from the French, restoring some of the losses his ancestors had suffered in France (e.g. Poitou, Ponthieu, Montreuil), securing possession of Gascony without doing any homage to the king of France and a promise of a large ransom for the captive Jean II.

SC 13/K5 Edward III's 4th great seal of presence, obverse.

SC 13/K5 Edward III's 4th great seal of presence, reverse.

In his new seal, now known to historians as the 'Brétigny seal', Edward sits in the central of three arches on his canopied throne. At the top of the central arch is a small figure wearing a crown and holding up his right hand in blessing. This is a clear allusion to the favour God had granted to Edward in his endeavours. In each of the supporting arches is an oak tree, the symbol of solid lineage and enduring strength, with a bird in the branches and a greyhound, a sign of loyalty and of the hunt, the king's favourite pastime, at the foot. From each tree is hung a shield of

DL 10/324 Inspection of the grant to Edward de Bohun of the castle and peel of Lochmaben, Annandale and Moffatsdale (Dumfries-shire), sealed with the 'Bretigny seal' of Edward III, 1361, obverse.

arms with France quartering England. In narrow niches either side of the king are figures (on the viewer's left) of the Virgin Mary and Child and (on the right) the patron saint of England, St George. On the perimeter of the field are two figures of men-at-arms, figuratively protecting the king and alluding to his military successes with the whole community behind him. On the reverse, the king is in full war cry, himself and his horse adorned with heraldic dress. The perimeter of the seal is shaped by tracery as if to frame the king in further magnificence.

DL 10/324 Inspection of the grant to Edward de Bohun of the castle and peel of Lochmaben, Annandale and Moffatsdale (Dumfries-shire), sealed with the 'Bretigny seal' of Edward III, 1361, reverse.

HENRY IV (1399-1413)

If we are looking for arguably the finest example of the seal-maker's art in the Middle Ages, though, one which develops the iconographical meaning and arrangement to new levels, we need search no further than the new great seal cast for Edward's grandson, King Henry IV, in 1406.

By this time, Henry had a more secure hold on the throne he had usurped from his cousin Richard II in 1399, having survived a series of rebellions early in his reign but now needing further to prove his legitimacy and so tie his kingship

E 42/488 Grant by Richard II to John Montagu, earl of Salisbury, of the manors of Kenninghall (Norfolk) and Kessingland (Suffolk), 1398, Great Seal, obverse.

E 42/488 Grant by Richard II to John Montagu, earl of Salisbury, of the manors of Kenninghall (Norfolk) and Kessingland (Suffolk), 1398, Great Seal, reverse.

to his dynasty and his nation. The majesty portrait intricately places the figure of the king within a framework of niches on which sit the patron saints of England, saints Michael the Archangel, George, Edward the Confessor and Edmund the King and Martyr. The king is protected by the very best the Heavenly Host could provide for a king of England, combining an archangel with the English royal house's most revered patron saints. At the foot of the throne are the arms of Prince Henry, the king's eldest son, as prince of Wales, duke of Cornwall and earl of Chester. The prince would himself continue to use this splendid seal until 1420 when the Treaty of Troyes cemented his military victories over the French and brought him the throne of France for himself and his heirs.

During much of the fifteenth century, the great seal of England retained many of the same features as that of Edward III and Henry IV. As dynastic conflict spiralled out of control during the Wars of the Roses between the houses of Lancaster and York, intricate nuances were added. Edward IV (1461-1483), for example, introduced dozens of tiny 'sun in splendour' motifs (circular sun

DL 10/373 Exemplification by Henry IV of a grant (originally dated to 1265) to Edmund of Lancaster of the honour of Lancaster, Newcastle under Lyme (Staffordshire), the honour of Pickering, and Scalby (Yorkshire), Godmanchester and rents from Huntingdon (Huntingdonshire), 1410, second Great Seal, obverse.

DL 10/373 Exemplification by Henry IV of a grant (originally dated to 1265)
to Edmund of Lancaster of the honour of Lancaster, Newcastle under Lyme
(Staffordshire), the honour of Pickering, and Scalby (Yorkshire), Godmanchester
and rents from Huntingdon (Huntingdonshire), 1410, second Great Seal, reverse.

with rays shining out from the centre) in the field of the equestrian side of his
seal. This referred to the parhelion that had apparently signalled his victory
over the forces of his rival King Henry VI (1422-1471) at Mortimer's Cross
in Herefordshire in 1461 and opened his way to the throne. Edward's brother,
Richard III (1483-1485), used the very same seal, and you can see the vigour

DL 10/392 Letters patent recording the grant for seven years to William Hussey, Chief Justice of the King's Bench, and others, of Little Barningham (Norfolk), with reversion to Pleshey college (Essex), 1485, Great Seal of Richard III, obverse.

with which he rides an athletic horse, visor of his helmet open, the very essence of a late medieval monarch.

Traditionally, if not wholly accurately, the death of Richard in battle at Bosworth and the accession of Henry VII (1485-1509) marks the end of the medieval period. It also signals the beginning of the Renaissance era, one in which a battle for the soul of the nation fused with revolutions in human thought and

DL 10/392 Letters patent recording the grant for seven years to William Hussey, Chief Justice of the King's Bench, and others, of Little Barningham (Norfolk), with reversion to Pleshey college (Essex), 1485, Great Seal of Richard III, reverse.

emotions across the globe, which transferred to art, particularly in capturing the individual. Throughout the next 250 years or so, the royal great seal, while still recognisable in medium and message from its medieval forebear, mixed realistic portraiture with novel allegory to reinforce the perceived position of the sovereign as the centre of the nation and, increasingly, the world.

Henry VIII has often been seen as the epitome of the Renaissance king, being a promoter of humanist learning and new approaches to art and portraiture.

E 344/22, p. 21 Illuminated image of Henry VIII from the Valor Ecclesiasticus.

However, in terms of the message Henry wished to send through his great seal, for much of his reign it remained, conversely, medieval in style.

Henry's second great seal, in use from c. 1532 to 1542, is similar in style to that of his forebears but with characteristic artistic tweaks to enhance that message. For example, on the obverse, the shields of arms of France and

England are placed on the outer perimeter of the seal rather than close to the throne. They are also surrounded by the Garter, that most royal of orders, established in 1348 by Edward III at the height of his continental successes, whose small number of members were bound to the king by ties of family and service. Behind Henry's throne within the inner rim of the seal are multiple oval-shaped devices containing alternately the (Tudor) rose of England and the fleur-de-lys of France.

E 329/475 The King to Edward Seymour, knight: Grant of an annuity of 50 marks, 1530-1, first Great Seal of Henry VIII, obverse.

E 329/475 The King to Edward Seymour, knight: Grant of an annuity of 50 marks, 1530-1, first Great Seal of Henry VIII, reverse.

Henry's adoption and promotion of the Tudor Rose symbol, demonstrating the fusion in his person (and, of course, that of his elder brother, Arthur, who tragically died in 1502) of the warring houses of Lancaster (through his father, Henry VII) and York (through his mother, Elizabeth of York), is one of the most potent motifs of the Tudor monarchy. On the reverse of his second great seal, Henry is depicted in medieval fashion, on horseback, charging warrior-like to the right with a large plume on his helmet, sword in hand, his horse with a richly decorated heraldic caparison. Over his shoulder is a Tudor Rose, unmissable for its size. At the horse's feet runs a greyhound wearing an heraldic collar to show

Henry's descent from the house of York. The greyhound, a symbol in use since at least the reign of Edward III, also symbolises the royal love of the hunt and the king's position as the faithful defender of the nation.

This took on extra meaning with the religious reforms of Henry's reign. Early in the reign, Henry acted as a bulwark of the Catholic faith against growing calls for reform across Europe. In 1521, Pope Leo X awarded him the title of 'Defender of the Faith' (*Fidei Defensor*). But when, as a consequence of his wish to divorce from Katherine of Aragon, Henry moved to make himself Supreme Head of the Church of England and remove his kingdom from a perceived subservience to Rome, he adopted the title to represent another interpretation of the faith he aimed to defend. Henceforth, on the great seals of the monarchs of England and, later, Britain, the title 'Defender of the Faith' is included in the legend: HENRICVS OCTAV[VS] DEI GRA[TIA] ANGLIE ET FRANCIE REX FIDEI DEFENSOR ET DOMIN[VS] HIBERNIE ('Henry the Eighth, by the grace of God king of England and France, Defender of the Faith, and lord of Ireland'). The later addition of the kingship of Ireland – rather than lordship – reflected statutes of the Irish and English parliaments in 1540 and 1541 by which Henry successfully asserted his claim.

Henry commissioned a third great seal in 1542, which you can see below. The symbolism remained essentially similar but the style made a revolutionary leap forward from the medieval to the Renaissance. On the obverse is a bearded, overweight but still magnificent king, the Henry VIII that will be most familiar to us all from period portraits. Likewise, on the reverse the charging warrior king is flanked by the Tudor Rose and accompanied by the greyhound. The principal differences come in the throne, which is now arched and topped with a canopy, the height of contemporary fashion. The legend on both sides of the seal is now more pregnant with meaning than ever before: HENRIC[VS] OCTAV[V]S DEI GRATIA ANGLIE FRANCIE ET HIBERNIE REX FIDEI DEFE[N]SOR ET I[N] TERRA[M] ECCLESIÆ A[N]GLICANE ET HIBERNICE SVPREMV[M] CAPVT ('Henry the Eighth, by the grace of God king of England, France and Ireland, Defender of the Faith, and in the land of the English and Irish Church Supreme Head'). This, of course, reflected the fullness of the Reformation he had begun to bring about in England and foreshadowed the turmoil that would come over the next two centuries.

While different in certain elements, notably the imagery on the reverse, this third great seal owes its inspiration to the golden seal (technically an engraved metal disk rather than a seal of gold, a twentieth-century replica copy of which survives at The National Archives) with which Henry sealed his part of

E 30/1025 Seal case, Henry VIII and Katherine of Aragon, back.

E 328/408 Letters patent granting John, earl of Oxford, licence to grant to Edward, earl of Hertford, a meadow called *Alburne meades* and a parcel of land called *Litelthanke*, the grange of Westbaron, and a close of land and pasture in lordship called *le Drove* (Somerset), late of the Witham Charterhouse, and meadows in Westbaron and Witham. Westminster (19 May 1544), third Great Seal of Henry VIII, obverse.

E 328/408 Letters patent granting John, earl of Oxford, licence to grant to Edward, earl of Hertford, a meadow called *Alburne meades* and a parcel of land called *Litelthanke*, the grange of Westbaron, and a close of land and pasture in lordship called *le Drove* (Somerset), late of the Witham Charterhouse, and meadows in Westbaron and Witham. Westminster (19 May 1544), third Great Seal of Henry VIII, reverse.

a perpetual peace treaty with King Francis I of France in 1527. Henry's seal, possibly designed by the artist Hans Holbein, set out to convey the same sense of majesty and destiny as that of Francis I – according to the legend on the reverse 'by the grace of God the most Christian king of the French'. The obverse of Henry's seal shows the enthroned, youthful king surrounded by the usual trappings of majesty but sat, as in his third great seal, on an arched throne. Flowers adorn the canopy and are supported from falling by Classical cherubs standing on vases either side of the throne. Under Henry's feet is a large Tudor rose, again supported by two cherubs. The reverse displays the arms of England and France quartered surrounded by the collar of the Order of the Garter and topped with an arched crown; five Tudor roses surround the shield of arms, a supreme expression of the bonds between nation and dynasty. A legend reads ORDINE IVNGVNTVR ET PERSTANT FOEDERE CUNCTA ('All things are joined by order and stand firm by treaty'). This is a direct response to the legend on Francis's seal which reads PLVRIMA SERVANTVR FOEDERE, CVNCTA FIDE ('Most things are preserved by treaty, everything by trust'). Both are lofty expressions of friendship and the faith each side would put into the peace after long years of negotiation. Of course, such ambitions would be short-lived.

PRO 30/226/65 Replica seal of the 'Golden Bulla' with which Henry VIII sealed the treaty of perpetual peace with France, 1527, obverse.

PRO 30/226/65 Replica seal of the 'Golden Bulla' with which Henry VIII sealed the treaty of perpetual peace with France, 1527, reverse.

The legacy Henry left for his children was hugely problematic. The premature deaths of his son and heir Edward VI (1547-1553) and his eldest daughter Mary (1553-1558) further entrenched the violent battle for the soul of the nation as Protestant reform struggled to hold back the Counter-Reformation movement sponsored by foreign powers.

KB 27/1150/2, rot. 1 Coram Rege plea roll, Portrait of Edward VI, 1549.

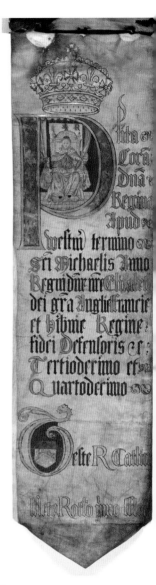

Above left: KB 27/1168/2, rot. 1 Coram Rege plea roll, Portrait of Mary I, 1553.

Above right: KB 27/1239, rot. 1 Coram Rege plea roll, Portrait of Elizabeth I, 1584.

Only under their sister Elizabeth I was the Protestant settlement consolidated, though not without considerable difficulty and paranoia in government circles. Throughout the Early Modern period, the symbolism used on royal great seals continued overtly to express political, religious and dynastic ambitions.

ELIZABETH I (1558-1603)

Of all the monarchs of England (and, indeed, Britain), it is perhaps Queen Elizabeth I who mastered the art of manipulation of imagery for political and personal purposes. Not only did she have to deal with the politicisation of faith and the duties of royal government but also to rule as a female monarch, which brought unique challenges that had to be overcome. Much of this is reflected in the imagery used on her great seals.

Elizabeth's younger brother Edward VI essentially adopted the imagery of his father's third great seal. As had been the case with King Henry III in the thirteenth century, the images of majesty and martial prowess on Edward's seal masked his youth and, in his case, ill health. In some senses, the great seal of his sister Mary had to be starkly different from that which had come before. The portrait of the enthroned queen with sceptre and orb is of long standing, though the throne and its canopy are less elaborate than those of her father and brother. Mary is flanked by the Tudor Rose and a crowned shield with the arms of France and England. Allan Wyon, the great Victorian scholar of royal great seals, unkindly described the image of Mary as 'very squat and ungainly' (Wyon, *The Great Seals of England*, p. 73). The craftsmanship of her great seal does not appear to be as fine as earlier Tudor examples, but she retains dignity and grace in her much under-appreciated portrayal despite cutting, for Wyon, 'a peculiarly ungraceful equestrian figure'. This is particularly so on the reverse where, instead of a warrior king, the queen had to fashion a new image of royal leadership. In this seal the queen wears her crown and trots towards the left on a muscular charger adorned with a large saddle-cloth which is decorated with a chequerboard of lozenges, each filled with either a castle or a pomegranate, the symbols of Mary's mother Katherine of Aragon. Other national symbolism is evident: behind the queen's shoulder is a large fleur-de-lys, while in front of the horse is a rosebush giving life to three roses.

Taking symbolism from her mother was one thing, but Mary's gender as monarch was a major political problem not only in England but also throughout Catholic Europe. The solution was to unite England through Mary with Spain in the person of Philip, son of the Holy Roman Emperor Charles V, a decade her junior.

Their marriage in 1554 effectively introduced a dual monarchy into England, hereditary authority being vested in Mary but some elements of policy lying with Philip. The transformation this necessarily wrought upon royal imagery was immense. The couple had a new great seal cut which on the obverse shows

DL 10/422 Letters patent annexing lands in cos. Hertfordshire, Essex,
Buckinghamshire, Suffolk, Sussex, Cambridgeshire and Yorkshire, to the
Duchy of Lancaster, great seal of Philip and Mary, 1558, obverse.

DL 10/422 Letters patent annexing lands in cos. Hertfordshire, Essex, Buckinghamshire, Suffolk, Sussex, Cambridgeshire and Yorkshire, to the Duchy of Lancaster, great seal of Philip and Mary, 1558, reverse.

KB 27/1185, rot. 1 Coram Rege plea roll, Portrait of Mary and Philip, 1558.

them, engraved in naturalistic style, enthroned next to each other, gazing at each other while both laying a hand on a large orb topped with a cross. The orb sits on a pedestal on which is depicted a crown and the letters 'P' and 'M' entwined in a knot. In his right hand, the king holds a sword in medieval fashion while the queen holds a sceptre in her left hand, a symbolic reflection of their perceived roles as military leader and fount of justice. Between the figures is a large shield in which the arms of Spain impale those of England. The very long legend reads PHILIP[PVS] ET MARIA D[EI] G[RATIA] REX ET REGINA ANGL[IE] HISPANIAR[UM] FRANC[IE] VTRIVSQUE SICILIE IERVSALEM ET HIB[ERNIE] FIDEI DEFENSOR[ES] ('Philip and Mary, by the grace of God king and queen of England, Spain, France, both parts of Sicily, Jerusalem and Ireland, Defenders of the Faith'). On the reverse, both figures are trotting left on elegantly engraved horses, and the monarchs are again respectively holding sword and sceptre. Mary rides side-saddle and gazes back towards Philip who wears not the full plate armour of his medieval predecessors but leather armour and a cap. Another double shield of arms appears surrounded by the Garter. The legend reads ARCHIDVCES AVSTRIE DVCES BVRGVNDIE MEDIOLANI ET BRABANCIE COMITES HASPVRGE FLANDRIE ET TIROLIE ('Archdukes of Austria, Dukes of Burgundy, Milan and Brabant, Counts of Hapsburg, Flanders and the Tirol'), which acknowledges the multiple European titles Philip brought to the match and the centrality to continental Catholicism of the marriage. The seal in its entirety symbolically emphasised the political and diplomatic alliance of England and Spain that would last only as long as the ailing queen, who died after only five years of wedlock.

Her successor, her younger sister Elizabeth, shattered all such pretensions and in her forty-five years as queen re-forged monarchy – and England – in her own image. Coming to the throne at twenty-five and unmarried, Elizabeth shared the difficulties of her sister in being a female monarch. For the first half of her reign, Elizabeth adopted a relatively conventional portrait on her first great seal. On the obverse, she sits crowned on a throne described by Wyon as resembling a bedstead with curtains left undrawn on either side. She holds the sceptre in her right hand while the orb rests, rather comfortably, on her knee. Flanking her throne on either side are the quartered arms of England surrounded by a garter. Rather difficult to pick out is a motto PVLCHRVM PRO PATRIA PATI, which essentially appears to be a bastardised version of the Latin verse 'Dulce et decorum est pro patria mori/It is beautiful to die for your country'. For Elizabeth, whose reign was increasingly riddled with Catholic plots to remove her from

SC 13/K43, First Great Seal of Elizabeth I, 1558-1586, obverse.

SC 13/K43, First Great Seal of Elizabeth I, 1558-1586, reverse.

the throne, and to take her life, as well as attempts to marry her off to various suitors for diplomatic ends, this rather publicly demonstrated her unwillingness to be bowed and that she stood both for the Protestant religious settlement and the kingdom of England.

The reverse of her first great seal largely repeats the imagery on Mary's first great seal, with the queen riding a prancing horse side-saddle with its heraldic saddle-cloth and flanked by the Tudor Rose and fleur-de-lys. When in 1586 the queen commissioned a new seal matrix, the first having become worn through use, the difference was marked and represented a revolution in portraiture and image-making. Here, we have Elizabeth as Gloriana, an image familiar from numerous famous portraits of the queen painted in her middle age. She wears the crown above curled hair, a ruff collar and a richly decorated gown, which to some extent matches the caparison of her horse beneath her. The horse prances through a field full of flowers and studded with roses and lilies. On either side of the queen are a crowned Tudor Rose before her and a harp behind her. This is the first time Ireland is iconographically represented on the great seal of England and reinforced the English claim to the kingship of Ireland during a century when English power and colonial government was being strongly reasserted.

For the first time, too, a space has been deliberately made on the outer rim which surrounds the crown of the queen's head but does not punctuate the legend. It is in the form of clouds from which (though again incredibly difficult to pick out) the sun's rays illuminate the queen in her full glory, a sign of favour from Heaven. This celestial blessing is repeated in more dramatic form on the obverse of this new seal as two arms stretch out from the edge of the seal to drape a furred mantle over the queen's shoulders. Elizabeth is crowned and wearing a large ruff collar and opulent, wide gown which all but obscures the throne on which she sits. On either side of her shoulders are two Tudor roses, while two shields of arms with crowns on top and surrounded by a garter fill out the remainder of the field on either side of the throne. Elizabeth has few matches in this portrayal of majesty.

The credit for this masterpiece goes largely to the renowned miniaturist Nicholas Hilliard, whose 'paternes' for a seal 'to be in forme as neare as may be vnto our said former Greate Seale' were to be engraved in the workshop of Dederick Anthony, graver of the royal mint. [SP 15/28, no. 86, warrant, 8 July 1584] Their combined effort makes Elizabeth I's second great seal an exquisite portrayal of a queen at the height of her and her nation's powers.

SC 13/N3, Second Great Seal of Elizabeth I, 1586-1603, obverse.

SC 13/N3, Second Great Seal of Elizabeth I, 1586-1603, reverse.

JAMES I (1603-1625)

Elizabeth died childless in March 1603. Her nominated successor was her kinsman and fellow monarch, King James VI of Scotland, upon whose accession to the English throne became King James I in that realm.

Initially, in the hurry to move south for a coronation, James adopted Elizabeth's matrix for formal acts under his warrant, it being committed to him at Broxbourne in Hertfordshire on 3 May. Within three months, though, James had a new great seal and caused Elizabeth's matrix to be defaced at Hampton Court. The visual impression Elizabeth's seal had apparently made on James during this short period compelled him to resort to Hilliard to design his great seal of state. Hilliard's designs were approved by 9 May, possibly before

KB 27/1522, rot. 1, Coram Rege plea roll, Portrait of James I, 1623.

James reached London, and the matrices finished by 19 July 1603. The result is another artistic gem full of allusive imagery: on the obverse James is enthroned and crowned and robed in the mantle and collar of the Order of the Garter. He is flanked by shields quartered with the arms of England, Scotland (lion rampant) and Ireland (harp), surrounded by the Garter. To the left of the throne is a crowned, seated lion representing England, bearing a banner with the arms of Cadwaladr, last king of the Britons, to the right a unicorn representing Scotland bearing the banner of the English royal saint Edward the Confessor. This is a highly nuanced portrayal of the union of the crowns of England and Scotland and the fusing of national imagery inherent in the person of a king of both realms. The equestrian portrait of James on the reverse returns to that of the last adult male monarch, Henry VIII, which sees James as a military figure charging in a field full of national symbolism (the crowned Tudor Rose, the Irish harp, the fleur-de-lys) and running alongside him the greyhound protector. Hilliard ensured this seal represented both modern realities and ancient heritage and claims.

James adopted a second seal in 1605 which essentially repeated the imagery Hilliard had created for him. His son Charles I (1625-1649) followed this lead, with subtle changes made across his four great seals.

Charles is the first monarch, for example, to bring the concept of Great Britain ('Magna Britannia') to his great seal in 1625, though this was quickly abandoned.

The second to fourth great seals of Charles also feature a superbly engraved miniature portrait of the London skyline between the galloping hooves of his horse on the reverse side and a ship on the River Thames.

It was under Charles that physical possession of the great seal became a political issue of the highest importance too. In 1640, with Charles in dispute with parliament over who held the reins of power, the keeper of the great seal fled London with the seal. Shorn of the ultimate authority for making grants and laws (for whatever can be said of the great seal's imagery its primary function was as an authority and validation for the king's will), parliament engaged in stormy debate about what should be done. Ultimately, in 1643, it passed resolutions that the great seal ought to reside with parliament and that the current great seal ought not to have legal force. This paved the way for a fourth great seal matrix to be cut that resided wholly with parliament and was never actively in royal hands. In 1646, the old great seal matrix was recovered and ceremonially broken in parliament to the cheers of members. This fate also awaited the new fourth great seal matrix, which bore imagery of the king, when a week after the execution of Charles in Whitehall on 30 January 1649, his final seal was smashed into fragments.

SC 13/N4, First Great Seal of James I, 1603-1605, obverse.

SC 13/N4, First Great Seal of James I, 1603-1605, reverse.

KB 27/1681, rot. 1, Coram Rege plea roll, Portrait of Charles I, 1643.

E 156/6, Letters patent concerning Queen Henrietta Maria's settlement, first Great Seal of Charles I, 14 March 1627, obverse.

The political revolution wrought by parliament in 1649 was reflected in the revolutionary design of the great seal used during the Interregnum. Royal insignia and imagery were stripped away and replaced, on the obverse, with a map of England, Wales and Ireland (Scotland having a separate parliament). Aspirations towards English/British naval supremacy, and an emphasis on the insular aspect of the nation, are displayed by several ships in the key channels of

E 156/6, Letters patent concerning Queen Henrietta Maria's settlement, first Great Seal of Charles I, 14 March 1627, reverse.

the North Sea. Two large oval shields are placed in the upper and lower halves, one bearing the arms of St George and the other the Irish harp. The levelling nature of parliamentary government is perfectly rendered in an engraving on the reverse of parliament in session, with the Speaker presiding. The legends are very stark and pointed: THE GREAT SEALE OF ENGLAND 1648/IN THE FIRST YEARE OF FREEDOME BY GOD'S BLESSING RESTORED 1648. They accentuate the republican notions of popular liberty and common endeavour inherent in the revolution.

Despite his leadership of the campaign which overthrew Charles I and his commitment to republican ideals, Oliver Cromwell restored elements of majesty and military might to the great seal commissioned to mark his protectorate of England from 1655, and subsequently adopted by his son Richard to the Restoration in 1660. On the obverse, the Protector's seal bears a quartered shield with the arms of St George top left and bottom right, the saltire of St Andrew top right and the Irish harp bottom left. The arms are supported by a crowned lion and a griffin. A motto reads PAX QUAERITVR BELLO ('Peace is sought by battle'), a clear allusion to Cromwell's successful leadership of the Republic. On the reverse, Cromwell restores the equestrian image. He wears armour adorned with a sash but no helmet. A shield with a lion rampant in the centre – the Cromwell arms – figuratively ties the Protector to the nation(s). Cromwell also continues with the device of the London riverscape which first appeared under Charles. The legend confirms the new state of affairs but also affirms the central place of Cromwell within the state and religious culture of the nation: MAGNUM SIGILLUM REIPUB[LICÆ] ANGLIÆ SCOTIÆ ET HIBERNIÆ &cte ('Great seal of the Republic of England, Scotland and Ireland etc.') on the obverse; and OLIVARIUS DEI GRA[TIA] REIP[UBLICÆ] ANGLIÆ SCOTIÆ ET HIBERNIÆ &c PROTECTOR ('Oliver, by the grace of God Protector of the Republic of England, Scotland and Ireland etc.')

When royal authority was restored in 1660 with the return from his continental exile and subsequent coronation of Charles II (1660-1685), the essential pattern of majesty and equestrian portraits was also restored. Throughout his period in exile from England, Charles had retained a great seal matrix modelled on those of his father and grandfather, which he used for personal, royal business rather than business of state. During his reign, Charles used three great seals, each of which refined the majesty and equestrian images. Here in his fourth and final great seal, in use from 1672 to his death in 1685, is the final expression.

This Charles is instantly recognisable from contemporary portraiture: on the obverse his long, curled hair flows from beneath his crown, and he sits in a lavish canopied throne holding the regalia and flanked by the heraldic seated lion of England and unicorn of Scotland, now with a collar around its neck; on the reverse, the neatly-coiffured king skilfully handles a rearing warhorse harnessed with heraldic saddle-cloth and again bestriding a riverscape of London, while

PRO 30/24/33/11: Great Seal of England, 1651, obverse.

PRO 30/24/33/11: Great Seal of England, 1651, reverse.

SP 108/388, Fourth Great Seal of Charles II, 1672, obverse.

SP 108/388, Fourth Great Seal of Charles II, 1672, reverse.

Charles, clad in a cloak fastened at the shoulder in Roman fashion, grips a long, straight sword pointed slightly downwards. This vision is a powerful evocation of Charles, the warrior king in the Classical mould.

It would be an image several of his successors adopted, even when the Stuart royal line was extinguished with the death of Queen Anne (1702-1714) in 1714 and its replacement by the Hanoverians from northern Germany. Classical, mythical imagery began to compete with heraldic symbols on the great seals of what in 1707, with the formal union of the kingdoms of Scotland and England, would become Great Britain. The equestrian portraits on the great seals of William III (1688-1702) and George II (1727-60) are superb examples of this fusion of traditions, both men being the epitome of Classical generals in their cloaks, close-fitting armour and tunics, George even riding without stirrups to display his prowess in the saddle. These would be apt portraits of, respectively, the man whose successful invasion and war against James II won the kingdom, and the last British monarch to lead his troops into battle at Dettingen in 1743.

Of course, this kind of image was not always suitable. William III ruled in right of his wife, Queen Mary II (1688-1694), daughter of the exiled James II. Female rulers had to be presented somewhat differently, as we have seen. It is noticeable that the great seal of William and Mary, in use until her death in 1694, after which William reigned alone, is very reminiscent of the previous example of co-rulers in England, Philip and Mary, in the 1550s. The majesty portrait, indeed, of the two monarchs enthroned side by side, William bearing a sword, Mary bearing the sceptre, while both touch an orb placed on a pedestal inscribed with the letters 'G' (for 'Gullielmus', Latin for William) and 'M' (for 'Maria', Latin for Mary), bears a very striking (and probably deliberate) resemblance. The royal arms are, not unnaturally, different. William's own lion rampant of Nassau now features, while no reference is made to the arms of Scotland, the royal couple not being declared king and queen until some time after this seal had been fashioned. On the reverse, Mary almost appears an afterthought. She rides a little ahead of William, looking back towards him, but both she and her horse are almost totally obscured.

Queen Anne, Mary's sister and ultimate successor, brought her femininity and female power to the fore, however, in a manner similar to that of Elizabeth I. The imagery on her great seals changed radically as the political situation changed. Upon her accession, Anne's first great seal, in use to 1707, portrays the queen in standard Stuart majesty. The slender queen sits crowned on a canopied throne, at the top of which is a cherub blowing a trumpet with one hand and holding a moulding depicting the royal arms. At either side of her throne are two carved

T 40/1D Great Seal of William and Mary, 1692, obverse.

T 40/1D Great Seal of William and Mary, 1692, reverse.

ADM 224/1 Great Seal of George II, 1752, obverse.

ADM 224/1 Great Seal of George II, 1752, reverse.

female figures, one holding a church to represent piety and the other holding a pair of scales to represent justice, the essential qualities of female monarchy. The seated, crowned lion and seated, collared unicorn of, respectively, England and Scotland flank her feet. On the reverse the rather jaunty Anne, wearing what appears to be a winged bonnet on her head and a mantle and gown, rides side-saddle towards the left, holding a sceptre in her left hand.

T 40/4 Second Great Seal of Anne, attached to Treasury commissions of 1702, obverse.

T 40/4 Second Great Seal of Anne, attached to Treasury commissions of 1702, reverse.

It is this image which is radically reimagined on Anne's second great seal, commissioned in 1707 to mark the formal union of the kingdoms of Scotland and England, ratified by both parliaments that year (though, as you can see, there are changes to the arms and mythical beasts on the majesty side). Gone is the equestrian figure. Instead, the reverse of this seal features a seated figure of Britannia, that mythical woman of power who had appeared on English coinage since the 1670s and increasingly came to represent an outward-looking, island commonwealth of nations (England, Scotland and Ireland) that aspired to rule the waves and aggressively expand its influence over the globe. Dressed in Classical attire, Britannia sits against a rocky backdrop. In her right hand she holds a spear while her left rests upon an oval-shaped shield depicting the arms of England and Scotland. To the left of Britannia are a rose and a thistle growing from one stem, which is topped with a crown – the allusion here to the fusion of kingdoms into one nation could not be stronger. Britannia is surrounded by the legend BRITANNIA ANNO REGNI ANNÆ REGINÆ SEXTO ('Britain, the sixth year of the reign of Queen Anne').

Anne's second great seal is possibly the most impressive statement of female authority to have had wide circulation until the long reign of Queen Victoria (1837-1901) in the nineteenth century. Victoria, of course, could not only boast of regal authority over the constituent nations of Great Britain and (after the Act of Union of 1800/1) Ireland but also of a burgeoning, worldwide Empire and its millions of people. In her third great seal, in use from 1878, Victoria, gives us a portrait of magnificence in the Gothic Revival style.

In some senses, Victoria retained traditional modes of display. The equestrian image of the queen is similar in style to those of her female predecessors, in that she rides a prancing horse towards the left while wearing state robes and bearing the state regalia. A major difference here is the male groom who guides the horse. Maintaining the Classical style of the seal, he wears a short Roman-style tunic. On the majesty side of the seal, Victoria sits enthroned in long, flowing coronation robes with the collar and badge of the Order of the Garter while holding the orb and sceptre. But her throne is now covered with a fabulous Gothic-arched canopy and is approached by carpeted steps. Panels at the back of the throne display, in niches, a figure in a long robe holding a book and a bishop in his robes holding his pastoral staff in one hand and raising his other hand in benediction, a very medieval ecclesiastical image, as we will see in Chapter 3. The queen also no longer faces front; her body is angled slightly away from the viewer. She is attended – in a more pictorial development of Anne's second great seal – by two female figures: on the queen's left is the figure representing Religion, a woman wearing a headscarf and holding a thin cross-staff in one hand and a Bible in the other; on Victoria's right is Justice, a woman holding scales in her left hand and a drawn sword that points downwards in the other, the sword of truth. There is also no legend on this side, the text being replaced by a wreath of roses, rosebuds and thorns, oak leaves and acorns. This is a vision of a queen very much in tune with, and in many ways representative of, a society that valued faith and, gradual, improvements in social justice while revelling in medieval splendour.

C 110/26 Second Great Seal of Anne, 1711, obverse.

C 110/26 Second Great Seal of Anne, 1711, reverse.

HO 124/25 Warrant for the marriage of Princess Marie of Edinburgh and Prince Ferdinand of Romania, Third Great Seal of Queen Victoria, 1892.

These figurative Classical allusions are also borrowed from Victoria's Hanoverian ancestors and reflect British ambitions and world-view. In his first great seal, for example, the enthroned George III (1760-1820) is flanked by mythical figures – Justice, Piety, Plenty, the Roman Hercules and Minerva, gods of war, wisdom, art and learning, as well as Britannia. Similar imagery can be seen on the great seal of his son, George IV (1820-1830).

In practical terms the use of the great seal was limited from the eighteenth century onwards. In the early nineteenth century, sheriffs could be appointed

T 40/12 **First Great Seal of George III, 1782, reverse.**

T 40/12 First Great Seal of George III, 1782, obverse.

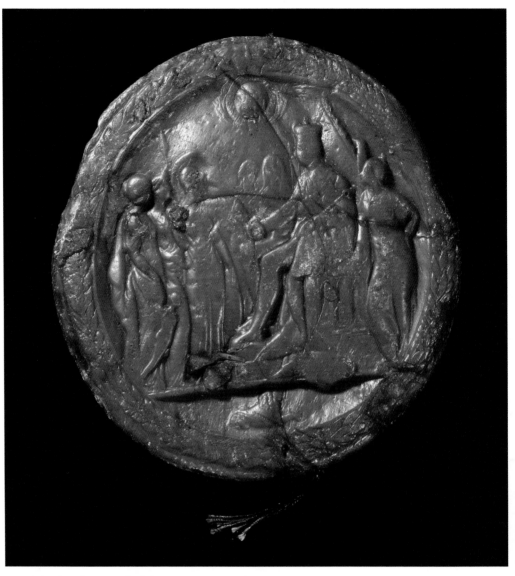

T 40/37 Great Seal of George IV, 1823, obverse.

by letters patent under the great seal until 1833. By 1883, a new Patent Office, the institution which dealt with the registration of new inventions, had received its own seal under the control of the Comptroller General of Patents. The use of the great seal, and of seals more widely, had been on the wane as a method of authentication and validation since the fifteenth century as the signature gained more currency. Initially, for a couple of centuries on legal transactions, both seal and signature were used by most parties, but gradually as written records proliferated, sealing lost its primary position. Nevertheless, for the most ceremonial pieces of royal business the great seal retained – and retains – a place in administrative culture and ritual.

The twentieth- and twenty-first-century monarchy, while increasingly modern in outlook, blended both ancient and modern symbolism in the production of its great seals. Perhaps the best example is the great seal of George V (1910-1935). Here we have a naturalistic portrait of George in majesty – the advent of photography and advertising brought the royal family into ordinary people's homes as never before – on the obverse, seated on a Gothic throne surrounded by the paraphernalia of ancient royal ritual and royal heraldry. On the reverse, though, George, the king who had led his country into and through the horrors

HO 124/41 First Great Seal of George V, 1923, obverse.

HO 124/41 First Great Seal of George V, 1923, reverse.

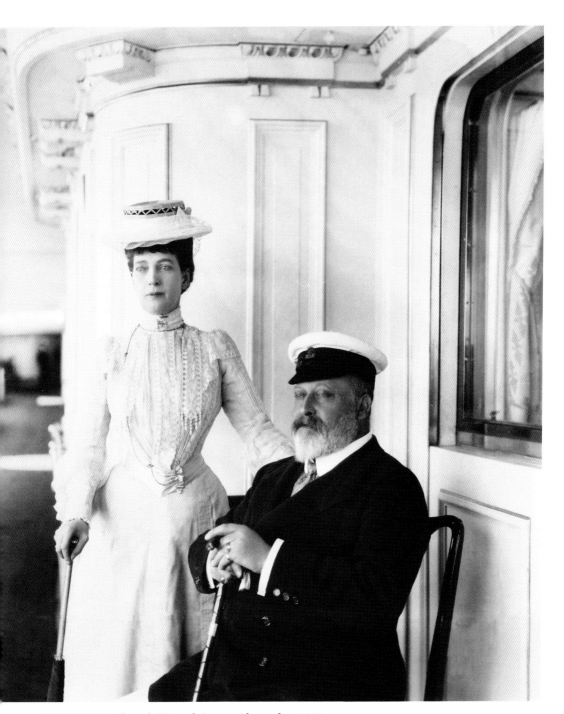

COPY 1/464 Edward VII and Queen Alexandra, 1903.

COPY 1/466 Image of George as Prince of Wales, 1903.

of the Great War, stands proudly in his naval officer's uniform at the prow of his ship. This represents a radical image of a military monarch and is a reminder of the king's personal pride in his naval training and position as Commander-in-Chief of the Armed Forces.

George VI (1936-1952), however, returns to a slightly more ancient form of military image in his great seal. Here, George is depicted on horseback, like his forebears going back to the Conquest wearing the period uniform of an officer with the plumed hat.

HO 125/16 Great Seal of George VI, 1948, obverse.

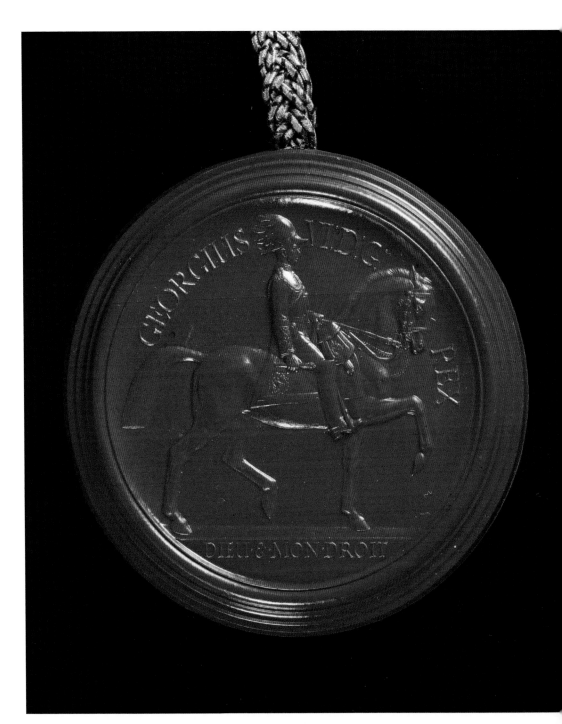

HO 125/16 Great Seal of George VI, 1948, reverse.

INF 3/78 Colour portrait of George VI, 1939-46.

His daughter, Elizabeth II (1952-present), the reigning queen, has not messed with tradition either. The majesty portrait on her first great seal, in use until 2001, is a very traditional image of the crowned, enthroned queen, sat with the regalia on the high-backed coronation chair in use since the early fourteenth century. On the equestrian reverse side, the queen, a noted horsewoman, is pictured trotting to the left in her ceremonial military uniform complete with a cap with a plume of feathers. Her personal monogram 'E.R.' (*Elizabetha Regina*) appears between the horse's hooves. In 2003, a new great seal was commissioned which depicts the royal arms on the reverse. Its function is now to authenticate letters patent, issue proclamations and commissions and to give force to some writs for parliamentary elections. The queen also ceremonially grants powers by her great seal to draw up and ratify treaty documents.

For almost one thousand years, the monarchs of England, Scotland and, later, Great Britain have symbolically given their assent to a vast array of royal, national and international business by authorising the attachment of an impression of their image made in a variety of media to written records. These complex images aimed to convey the power, majesty and continuous descent of individuals within the (supposedly) enduring institution of monarchy. For many centuries, the presentation and re-presentation of the sovereign in the great seal and its derivatives has radically shaped visual culture in Britain and latterly around the world. Generations of artists, particularly portraitists, have taken their inspiration from these subtle, nuanced images. Not unnaturally, both in terms of the legal, administrative functions and the creation of personal image, royal sealing practices have had a deep impact on all sections of society since the eleventh century, as we will see, albeit much more briefly, in the next chapter concerning Personal Seals.

CHAPTER 2

PERSONAL SEALS

This book mainly looks at the seals of kings and queens. However, their use of seals from the Middle Ages onwards as the primary means of authenticating and validating legal, financial and personal transactions in writing gradually promoted the practice throughout much of the rest of society. First, men and women of noble status followed the crown's lead. Then, as the use of writing spread, and written records took on greater authority as evidence, so ownership of a seal – or at least access to a seal – inevitably became an expected tool in the everyday lives of many people, men and women alike. Before the signature, seals were important for transferring land or property, undertaking business or showing assent to the activities of social superiors or peers. The seal became a key part of an individual's identity and status or – in modern terms – personal brand. And naturally, as the use of seals increased, so the variety of means and the range of motifs by which people wished their personal identity to be displayed increased. In this chapter, we will look in a little more detail at how men and women of diverse social groups used seals, particularly in the Middle Ages.

Almost as soon as the two-sided great seal started to become the principal mechanism by which the crown communicated its wishes to the community at large, so the elite nobility – the peers of the realm – adopted the seal for the same purposes. In the century or so after the Norman Conquest, the new Norman aristocracy in England, earls and leading barons, developed increasingly sophisticated designs for their seals that reflected their participation in the growing chivalric, military culture of medieval Europe, where display and magnificence were highly valued. In addition, members of the Anglo-Norman noble community transferred elements of this culture to Wales and Ireland (as well as the kingdom of Scotland) as the dominions claimed by the crown of England extended westwards. Even by the middle of the twelfth century, moreover, the lower nobility, lesser barons and knights, had begun to follow their social superiors.

Generally, the design of choice for your discerning twelfth-century magnate was – like the king – the equestrian portrait of the armoured knight on horseback, sporting a helmet, shield (which over time started to show his coat-of-arms as the mark of distinction and descent) and sword, lance and/or banner. This, of course, also like the king, meant that noble great seals were usually round to accommodate the horse and legend around the circumference, though usually they were slightly

DL 27/296: Grant in free alms by Walter de Lacy, lord of Meath, to the church and monks of St. Lawrence, Beybeg, of the church of St Patrick, Trim (Co. Meath, Ireland), 1216x1241, obverse.

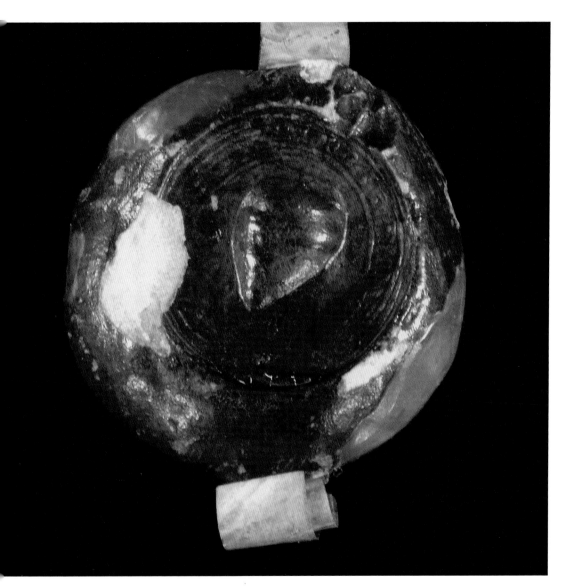

DL 27/296: Grant in free alms by Walter de Lacy, lord of Meath, to the church and monks of St. Lawrence, Beybeg, of the church of St Patrick, Trim (Co. Meath, Ireland), 1216x1241, reverse.

smaller than the king's at 4.5-8cm. The sight of the dashing charger and the rider equipped with the latest military fashions and hardware personified the owner and his caste like very little else and powerfully and dexterously conveyed how he wanted others to perceive him particularly in terms of social status and skills in combat. Some seals, like that of Walter de Lacy, lord of Meath in Ireland, are sealed on the reverse with a small counterseal bearing his arms.

One interesting departure from this is the seal imagery of the de Montfort family who claimed the earldom of Leicester in the thirteenth century. Successive counts and their sons eschewed the image of the knight on horseback and replaced it with the lord out hunting on his horse, blowing a horn and accompanied by his dogs. No armour or weaponry is in sight. This was not unique to the de Montforts either, as several lords preferred to display their nobility and status as a major landholder through a passion for noble sports rather than their military finery.

Similarly, though, other means were found of displaying key markers of noble birth, lineage and identity through the seal, often on the reverse. Heraldry, the system of unique combinations of colours, shapes and animals and birds, real and mythical, developed in the twelfth century to identify men on the field of combat whose faces were covered and also, as we've seen, to create and then accentuate individual identity within an accepted framework. The appearance and ultimate proliferation of heraldic devices on seals first developed on the carefully engraved surcoats (the tabard worn over the armour often in tournaments), pennons, saddlecloths and shields that adorn the rider on equestrian imagery. Quite quickly though, single devices or simple shields of arms (which developed over time as the heraldic system matured to cope with the intricacies of medieval intermarriage and the consequent shifts in the make-up of the upper classes) replaced or accompanied an equestrian image on seals. This replicated the developments witnessed with the royal deputed seals as we saw in Chapter 1. Technically, seals which display any kind of heraldic device are known as 'armorial', i.e. they bear the arms of an individual to display their identity and status.

The heraldic lion, whether prancing (known as 'passant') or rearing to an upright stance on its back legs and growling (known as 'rampant'), displayed the qualities of strength, nobility, ferocity and fighting ability to which many men aspired and so became a very popular symbol to add to noble seals. Leading families to adopt them included the Bigod earls of Norfolk and the de Blundeville earls of Chester and Lincoln.

In time, where the same design, whether identical or slightly nuanced to reflect better artistry or changing tastes, was used by particular people or families, this basic image would develop and become the inherited coats of arms. Still today, this is one of the chief markers of lineage or group identity, even though access to them is now wider and can be bought. Seal commissioners, designers and engravers may not have tinkered too much with the essentials of the imagery we've talked about during the Middle Ages, but they were obliged to be dedicated followers of fashion (if they weren't themselves innovators). One of the most stunning examples in The National Archives' collection is the great

E 26/2 Lion rampant emblem of Roger Bigod, earl of Norfolk, 1301.

seal of John de Warenne, sixth earl of Surrey (1231-1304). Originally attached to two copies of a letter from the leading barons of England to Pope Boniface VIII in 1301, which complained about the Pope's support for the Scots in their conflict with Edward I, this two-sided seal shows John in full battle array on the obverse. The earl wears his heraldic surcoat of azure blue and gold checks, while his charger is adorned in a large, flowing saddle-cloth and caparison of the same livery. Around the edge the legend reads '+ SIGILLVM IOHANNIS [C]OMITIS DE WARENNIA' ('Seal of John, earl of Warenne'). On the reverse of this seal, with a diameter of about eight centimetres, is his shield of arms set within an eight-leafed (or octofoil) design inlaid with flowers and foliage.

Earl Warenne's seal is a top-of-the-range example of the seal-maker's art in medieval England crafted from expensive, imported material such as the red dye vermilion that makes it sparkle. It is a mesmerising expression of an individual at the top of society who wanted the viewer to appreciate his status and breeding, wealth and taste as well as his military standing as one of Edward I's senior commanders during his recent conflicts with the Welsh and Scots. From around the middle of the thirteenth century, though, we find heraldic surcoats appearing over armour and the barrel helmet replacing the conical headpiece of earlier generations. By the fifteenth century, the adjustable visor made a regular appearance. As with royal shields, whereas in early examples the viewer could not see the front of the knight's main means of deflection and protection in combat, by the end of the twelfth century more and more men wanted the unique devices on their shields to be shown to the recipient of their written, sealed benefaction or instruction. The Earl Warenne was therefore simply trying to keep up with, if not ahead, of fashion.

However, as the use of heraldic devices on armorial seals increased with the number of individuals able and willing to display their status in this way, so members of the aristocratic elite followed the king in adopting a secondary seal, usually known as their privy or secret seal and sometimes set with a gemstone as a personal counterseal. This was not a trend which passed and the more personal privy (or secret) seal remained in vogue throughout the Middle Ages and across the British Isles as the example of the seal of Gerald fitz Maurice, earl of Desmond, from 1369-70 shows. Here, the earl acknowledges he has received a small part of his fee granted annually by the king for keeping the lordship of Ireland by having his privy seal attached to a thin tongue of parchment. His seal fuses two heraldic devices, the central shield of arms bearing the FitzGerald saltire, tying him into his conquistador lineage in Ireland.

E 26/1, no. 57: Seal of John de Warenne, sixth earl of Surrey, 1301, obverse.

E 26/1, no. 57: Seal of John de Warenne, sixth earl of Surrey, 1301, reverse.

E 213/169i: Receipt by Gerald fitz Maurice, earl of Desmond, to the Exchequer of Ireland, for £30 17s. 8d., part of his yearly fee of £500, with seal attached.

More spectacularly still, at the apex of noble society sat the royal family. Before usurping Richard II's throne in 1399, Henry of Bolingbroke (1367-1413), son of John of Gaunt and grandson of Edward III, owned a richly complex heraldic seal. Attached to a formulaic document appointing attorneys to act for Henry, the earl of Derby, Hereford and Northampton and lord of Brien, to receive possession of lands in Brecon in the marches of Wales, is a seal bearing a shield of arms with the old arms of France and England quartered (to demonstrate his royal lineage), with a label of five points (essentially a bar with five spikes at the top of the shield to show his place within the royal family). The shield hangs from a helm topped with a crest and a cap of estate showing a crowned leopard. On either side is the earl's personal insignia, the ostrich feathers, first adopted by his uncle Edward of Woodstock, the Black Prince, as a tribute to John,

DL 27/310: Appointment by Henry of Lancaster, earl of Derby, of John ap Henry, Thomas ap David, and Watkyn Wogan as attorneys to receive seisin of the town and castle of Bronllys, a third of the lands and fees of Cantref Selyf and Pencelli (Brecon), 1394, seal.

blind duke of Bohemia who perished at the battle of Crécy in 1346. The ostrich feathers still form part of the insignia of the heir to the throne and are used by Prince Charles today.

So far, we have really only talked about men and their seals. But throughout the Middle Ages women too sealed written transactions, whether as single women, wives or widows, businesswomen or landladies; generally speaking, married women could not act at law without their husbands but there are numerous examples within The National Archives' collection of seals owned by women.

In practical terms, the seals of elite women are similar to those of their male counterparts in that they are the personification in wax of an individual's status, gentility, education and taste. From the middle of the twelfth century, aristocratic ladies are most frequently depicted standing wearing fine long gowns, holding meaningful symbols in their hands.

Some women are depicted with a bird, usually a hawk or falcon, on their arm. This pointed to their skill in managing hunting birds and was a sign of their nobility. It can be seen here, in this important but faded seal of the Lincolnshire widow Nicholaa de la Haye, lady of Brattleby, who famously, as hereditary constable of Lincoln Castle, led the defence for the child King Henry III in the 1217 Battle of Lincoln against the baronial forces rallying to Prince Louis of France.

Other women are often shown holding a flower, possibly a lily, a symbol of female purity associated with the Virgin Mary, or a book, a marker of learning and erudition. One of the very finest examples is this seal from c. 1300 of Elizabeth, daughter of King Edward I, countess of Holland. Portrayed in expensive red wax, the countess could clearly afford to commission the best craftsmen to represent her image. Wearing a long, fine gown and head-dress, Elizabeth stands on a corbel of three pointed arches; her right hand grasps gently at her dress while on her left wrist sits a hawk. In the cross-hatched field behind and on either side of her are two shields of arms, the lion rampant of her late husband's county of Holland and her father's arms of the three lions *passant guardant* of England, a perfect heraldic representation of the union of two of Europe's most important comital and royal houses, respectively. The legend on her seal graphically outlines her status and titles: '+ S[IGILLUM] ELYSABETE COMITISSE HOLLANDIE ZELANDIE + D[OMI]NE FRISIE +', ('+ Seal of Elizabeth Countess of Holland [and] Zeeland + Lady of Frisia +'). On the reverse is a small counterseal bearing the lion rampant shield of arms of

DL 25/127: Quitclaim of the right of Desiree, daughter of Ermulf son of Alulf
in a house of her mother, Denise against the cemetery wall of St Paul's, London,
1201-1266.

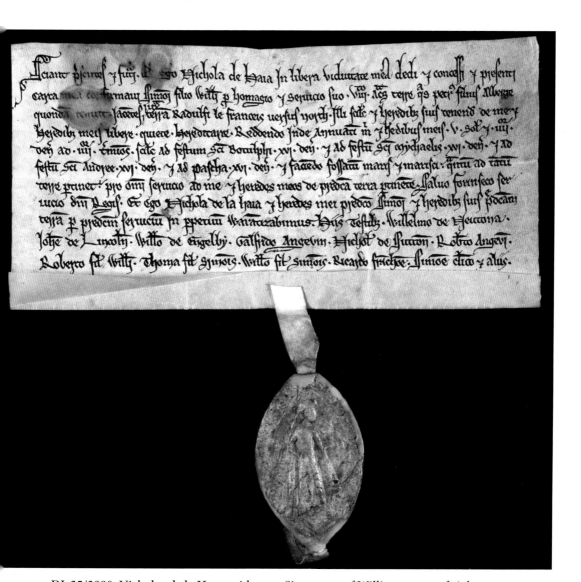

DL 25/2890: Nicholaa de la Haye, widow, to Simon son of William, grant of eight acres of land late of Peter son of Alberge, c. 1200-1235, with seal.

Holland and the legend '+ S[IGILLVM] SECRETI E[LIZABETHE] COMITISSE HOLLANDIE +', ('+ Secret seal of E[lizabeth] Countess of Holland +'). This, of course, demonstrates that Elizabeth had a privy seal with which she could authenticate more private, personal business if she so desired.

Seals of elite women tend to be in the shape of an oval, technically known as a 'vesica'. This was the ideal format in which to show the standing figure;

Above left: SC 13/F151: Seal of Elizabeth, countess of Holland and Zeeland, lady of Frisia, c. 1300, obverse.

Above right: SC 13/F151: Seal of Elizabeth, countess of Holland and Zeeland, lady of Frisia, c. 1300, reverse.

non-royal women would rarely, if ever, be pictured on horseback. As the medieval period continued, and the seal-owning population expanded, heraldry appeared more and more on women's seals, whether in the form of decorated gowns or in shields of arms showing their paternal descent or marital relationships. Some women are even shown holding shields of their arms.

Talk of widening the social spectrum on which people would hold seals brings us to by far the largest number of surviving seal impressions – those of non-elite men and women. The tens of thousands of examples at The National Archives dwarf the other collections. These range from those of gentlemen and women through merchants and those dwelling in towns and cities to the upper levels of the free peasantry in communities throughout these islands. Urban expansion, the development in the thirteenth century of the common law, complex trading and debt and credit relationships and the growth of the land market and the need to authenticate and record transactions all contributed to the wider spread of seal ownership. Possibly connected with this was a desire from landowners, individuals or institutions, to encourage their tenants to adopt such legal practices to make their own tenure and lordship more legally sound. Some individuals were sufficiently affluent or well connected to commission and/or buy a seal matrix to their own specification while others had to choose from off-the-shelf designs. There is also some evidence of matrices being supplied by lords to tenants. More people still might loan the seal of another or explicitly rely on the seal of a better-known individual or of a local municipal or legal authority to corroborate their transactions if they believed their seal was not well known outside their local area. This would be made clear in the sealing clause of the written document by a phrase like '… since our seal is unknown to many, the seal of the mayor of the town of X has been appended to better corroborate this business'. It has been argued by some seal scholars that, ultimately, the use of a personal seal in legal business was not the most important thing, rather that the physical act of sealing a document with any seal before trustworthy witnesses who were imbued with legal and memorial authority was key.

The number of possible non-armorial images was large and ever expanding, and people were increasingly creative with their choices. In the first three decades of the thirteenth century, around sixty free peasants of the Lincolnshire marshland villages of Frieston and Butterwick all sealed an agreement with their lord Ranulf de Blundeville, earl of Chester and Lincoln. In it, they released to him land in West Fen in return for other communal rights to pasture their animals, cut turves and mow hay. Though now quite badly damaged, these seals, all impressed in natural, uncoloured beeswax, display a range of simple images that include flowers (especially lilies), wheels and other radial designs, crescents and stars.

DL 27/270: Agreement by which men of Frieston (Frestoun) and Butterwick, Lincolnshire, quitclaim to Ranulf [de Blundeville], earl of Chester and Lincoln lands etc. in West Fen in return for other common of pasture, turbary and mowing rights, for a specified hearth rent of two pence, c. 1217-1232, with multiple seals.

From around this time on, the range of animals on non-armorial seals expanded to encompass heraldic animals such as lions and birds, some naturalistic, others mythical like the phoenix, as well as common fauna like dogs, bears, wolves, rabbits and squirrels. Many animals were imbued with symbolic meaning during the Middle Ages or could be used as rebuses – puns on individual's names. Others had more subtle meaning, such as the commonly found squirrel nibbling at a nut with the legend 'I CRAKE NOTIS', a sign, apparently, of sexual conquest.

Similarly, flora flourished, so to speak, on seals. Lilies, roses, daisies and other foliate designs were widespread. Crops also make occasional appearances as in the c. 1460 seal of William Bacon which features a sheaf of corn and the legend 'BE IT AS GOD WYLL' [E 326/10068].

E 39/99/1, string 7: Stag's head, 1296.

Religious imagery not surprisingly constitutes another major branch of the body of non-armorial seals. While some people might associate themselves with their patron (or name) saint by depicting that saint or the implements of their martyrdom on their seal (it is perhaps for that reason, for example, that the wheel on which St Catherine was broken is so popular an image, although of course the wheel might also represent Fortune's Wheel and the unpredictability of life), others, particularly women and clerks, alighted on the Blessed Virgin Mary. There are innumerable examples of seals on which the crowned Virgin bears the Christ child, or on which a legend such as 'Ave Maria' or 'Mater Dei Memento Mei/Mother of God, remember me' might appear. Other religious imagery includes the pelican pecking at its breast – the so-called 'Pelican in its piety' – feeding its young from the outpouring of blood, which symbolised the sacrifice of Christ on the Cross, and the Agnus Dei, a ubiquitous image of the Lamb of God, Jesus Christ, bearing his banner. Some seal owners expressed their piety through legends too, the Latin recital of the four Evangelists '*Mattheus, Marcus, Lucas, Johannes*' being popular. Slightly more esoterically, one seal owner after the Reformation, Francis Bowyer, grocer of London, used a skull as his emblem, perhaps signifying his recognition of the transitory nature of life. [E 210/10665]

More practical imagery associated with the owner's occupation could also appear on seals. For businessmen, an easy way of advertising their skills was to commission a fine seal displaying the tools or output of their trade. So, for example, we find bellfounders being recognisable via a bell, tailors via shears or scissors and brewers via a beer vat.

Finally, though, it is worth remembering that many people would have used a seal matrix that they simply bought from a local retailer, many of which were crafted from lower quality materials. By the late Middle Ages and as recently as the nineteenth century, only those who regularly authenticated documents really needed to own a seal matrix themselves; others could simply borrow from friends, neighbours, scribes or legal officials if they needed to seal. As the fifteenth century progressed, and certainly by the sixteenth century, seals were increasingly used in connection with an individual's sign manual or signature if they were literate. We often find a signature written next to (or occasionally on) the seal tag. Gradually, this signalled the death knell of the seal for most members of society, although even into the twentieth century, the seal continued to carry legal force for many transactions. Only when letters or business documents needed closing for dispatch and privacy would the seal continue its use in any volume.

CHAPTER 3

ECCLESIASTICAL SEALS

Across western Europe in the Middle Ages, at least until the cataclysm of the Protestant Reformation in the sixteenth century but also far beyond, in many countries the temporal monarchy sat alongside the supposedly undying spiritual and legal authority of the Roman Catholic church. Religion vitally underpinned and informed almost every facet of human existence. Throughout these islands in the medieval period the Church was a major land and property owner, business dealer and tax collector; senior churchmen acted as counsellors of kings and government officials as well as the spiritual and administrative leaders at the top of a complex, hierarchical organisation of dioceses, archdioceses, deaneries and parishes. The Church also exercised spiritual and moral oversight of the people; church courts dealt with a vast array of offences against Canon Law, including non-payment of tithes, non-attendance at services, adultery, defamation and 'pollution' of sacred spaces, whether through the sacrilegious spilling of blood or physical incursions onto church precincts.

The business of administering the Church and the law was increasingly conducted in writing, for which, as with secular business, seals were required as guarantors of authenticity and validity. As early as 1237, a legate from the papacy, Otto, negotiated a series of 'constitutions' that dictated the future governance of the English Church, whose freedom from arbitrary secular intrusion had so recently been secured through Magna Carta of 1215 and its recension in 1225. A section concerned seals. It established that not only should archbishops and bishops have seals but so should their senior and lesser officials of cathedral chapters, the seats of the diocesan structure, and archdeaconries and rural deaneries, those men who exercised authority and organised church administration locally. Otto also laid out what it meant to have an 'authentic' seal: this should always name the institution or office and its holder if held permanently; temporary office holders, like rural deans, did not need to be named. The educated status of much of the clergy – though, of course, to differing degrees – imbued such men with literate authority locally.

Nevertheless, the institutional Church and its personnel were not the only members of the ecclesiastical community who required and used seals. Monastic foundations of men and women established to live as enclosed communities under rules that regulated prayer, worship, diet, lifestyle, business, you name it, which had spread gradually before the Norman Conquest, proliferated thereafter. Vast networks of monasteries emerged across these islands. Many were founded as daughter houses of continental monasteries, while others were founded under the patronage of monarchies, whose members looked to them for their intercessory power of prayer and innate holiness, learning and counsel. During and from the twelfth century, many monastic houses received benefactions in terms of land or annual payments from the nobility, keen to enjoy the same spiritual benefits as did kings from this kind of patronage. Conversely, some houses, particularly within the more austere Cistercian Order but actually throughout most orders, as well as members of the military orders of the Knights Templar and Knights Hospitaller, engaged in complicated business transactions, forward selling wool and grain for ready cash to fund vast building projects. Such a wide range of business demanded transactions in writing and therefore the widespread use of seals within the monastic context. This was even the case with the Cistercians, the statutes of which order had to be constantly updated to permit modifications in seal possession and design over the long thirteenth century. From 1200, Cistercian houses were not permitted to own a common seal, and an abbot should have only one seal with a simple design of the man himself with his crosier, the pastoral staff of office, or, as in this example from Stratford Langthorne in Essex, a crosier being grasped by a hand. The simple tree metaphor in the centre of this seal may represent the Tree of Life. Around the outside is the simple legend '+ SIGILLVM ABBATIS DE STRATFOR', ('+ Seal of the Abbot of Stratford').

Further amendments to statutes relating to English Cistercian houses allowed, in 1257, the abbot to have a counterseal for more private business, and, in 1307, all houses to have a common seal. The latter was passed by the parliament gathered at Carlisle in pursuit of Edward I's Scottish campaign and aimed at preventing money being sent outside the kingdom at a time both of military need and as several English Cistercian houses recovered from severe financial problems caused by disease and economic crisis in the previous decades that had seen many unable to fulfil sizeable wool contracts.

At the top of the ecclesiastical hierarchy in England, Wales, Ireland and Scotland (the Papacy, of course, exercising ultimate authority within the Roman Catholic

E 42/470: Confirmation by B., abbot of Stratford [Langthorne], of a gift by Geoffrey White of land held of him by Robert Gambun in the bishop of London's soke for the light before the high altar; with seal, early thirteenth century.

Church) stood the archbishops, who exercised jurisdiction over large provinces as metropolitans, and bishops who ran dioceses. Like kings, these men began using great seals – the episcopal 'seal of dignity' – from around the eleventh century, on the one hand to validate written transactions concerning the transfer of land and property, and on the other to express their assent to an expanding range of bureaucratic instruments. Such instruments related, for instance, to appointments to rectories and vicarages, church offices and licenses to preach, and to make official pronouncements and communicate royal edicts to their personnel and their flock.

Most seals of dignity display a beautifully engraved image of the (arch) bishop standing rigidly upright and facing towards the viewer. He wears full vestments – the archbishop would wear his Y-shaped woollen pallium around his neck to signify the superior dignity of his office conferred by the papacy – and his mitre, holds his pastoral crosier in the left hand and raises the index and middle fingers of his right hand in blessing. This image was largely unchanged throughout the medieval period and remained, like many seals of aristocratic women, couched within an oval, better to accommodate the standing figure. As an approximation, most episcopal seals are between six and eight centimetres in height and four to six in width. The legend would then fit clockwise around the perimeter.

Modifications to this classic image during the Middle Ages largely relate to the increasingly ornate and complex architecture behind and symbolism flanking the standing figure. Around the end of the twelfth century, foliage and flora, crosses and stars appear in the background, giving way within the thirteenth century to pointed-arch canopies and niches in the Gothic style. Saintly symbols like the keys of St Peter were similarly popular. These niches housed figures of saints, often either side of the central figure; this set the (arch)bishop within the framework of celestial blessing and in some cases of his saintly predecessors. Leading churchmen were also very often from aristocratic families and, consequently, personal and dynastic heraldry began appearing in the thirteenth century alongside arms relating to the diocese or particular office. During the fourteenth century some ecclesiastics removed themselves from the central location on their seals and portrayed themselves in miniature kneeling before a saintly figure, often the Virgin and Child, in prayer.

Protestant reformers attempted to break the power of the episcopacy, even abolishing it altogether in England during the seventeenth-century Civil War. The medieval mitred and robed figure was transformed into the bishop preaching or in prayer. Imagery on seals changed radically; saints were removed and replaced with Biblical imagery, often from the Old Testament, as in the seal of Robert Horne, bishop of Winchester, which has an image of Jonah being swallowed by a huge whale. [E 355/4]

Very much like kings and queens, once the (arch)bishop had either died or been transferred to another see, his seal matrix was supposed to be ceremonially broken; they were not supposed to act for their successors. However, leading churchmen had long used a secondary seal for more private correspondence (it might also be used during the period between election and consecration). These seals were often impressed into the reverse of their great seal and are known as counterseals. Some of the most important counterseals are also some of the most beautiful examples from the Middle Ages. Thomas Becket, the man who would be martyred as archbishop of Canterbury in 1170, for example, used a small seal, possibly set into a ring usually worn on the finger, featuring a tiny winged Mercury, the Roman messenger god. Thomas potentially used this as a symbol of his aspirations to wisdom and graceful speech and appearance. In so doing, he reflected the practice of some of his predecessors and peers; many churchmen started using Classical gemstones that displayed pagan imagery, busts of gods and goddesses being popular. It was perhaps part of their culture of erudition and learning that they sought association with Classical images and tropes and, in some cases, sought to emulate each other in their choice of gemstones to achieve this. Similarly, while gemstones could be acquired on the market in England, Rome was an obvious centre for their trade and where senior churchmen would perhaps visit during their careers.

SC 13/43: Seal of Robert Wishart, bishop of Glasgow, 1273x1316.

E 30/438: Truce between England and Castile for a year from 1 May next. Given in London. Seal of William Alnwick, bishop of Norwich, 1430.

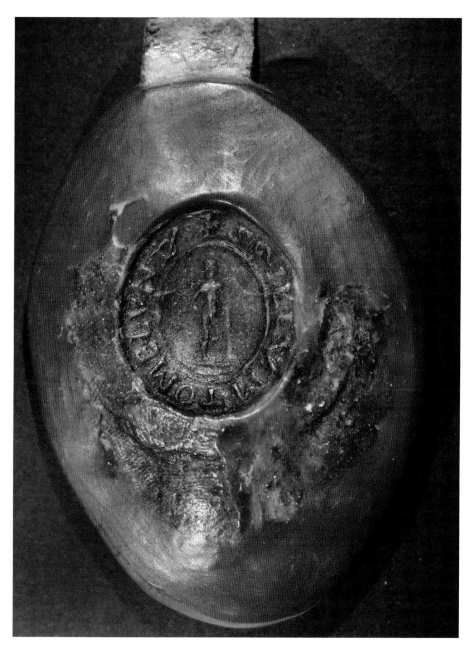

E 40/4913: confirmation in free alms, addressed to Walter, bishop of Rochester, by
Thomas [Becket], archbishop of Canterbury, to the canons of Holy Trinity, London,
of the church of St. Mary, Bickley [Kent], the grantor's predecessors, with lands
and tithes belonging to it, with license to have ten animals in the grantor's demesne
herbage, and ten hogs in his wood without pannage; counterseal of Archbishop
Becket in a cloth bag, c. 1162-70.

DL 27/4: Confirmation by S[tephen Langton], archbishop of Canterbury, of
the charter by Lewes Priory to Humphrey de Bohun and Maud, his mother,
concerning the election of priors of Farleigh (Wiltshire), which Archbishop
Hubert [Walter] had also confirmed, 1213-15, obverse of seal.

DL 27/4: Confirmation by S[tephen Langton], archbishop of Canterbury, of the charter by Lewes Priory to Humphrey de Bohun and Maud, his mother, concerning the election of priors of Farleigh (Wiltshire), which Archbishop Hubert [Walter] had also confirmed, 1213-15, counterseal.

One of Becket's successors as archbishop of Canterbury following his murder, Stephen Langton (1207-1228), used a counterseal that paid homage to the martyr and tied himself into the direct line of succession. On the reverse of a seal featuring the traditional standing figure of the archbishop on the obverse is a counterseal of similar size which shows the moment of Thomas Becket's martyrdom in Canterbury Cathedral by the four knights, Reginald fitz Urse, Hugh de Morville, William de Tracy and Richard le Breton. The kneeling figure of Becket is assailed by four standing figures brandishing their swords. One of the swords cuts off the top of Becket's head and a tiny piece of scalp – the corona – tumbles to the cathedral floor. That such a dramatic scene could be engraved with such precision is testament to the craftsmen at Langton's disposal and his pretensions and devotion to his saintly predecessor.

The practices of sealing adopted by archbishops and bishops was reflected throughout the clerical hierarchy due to the vast array of business the institutional church and its personnel had to deal with in managing the administration and enforcing religious laws. Sealing was therefore ubiquitous in clerical as much as it was in secular society, and, just as did laymen, so clerks sought seals of office and personal seals that were made of lower grade materials and shared the full range of possible images. Not surprisingly, traditional Christian imagery – saints (especially the Virgin and Child), the pelican in its piety, the Agnus Dei, simple or more complex crosses, for example – were paired with Biblical and other Christian mottoes. Many clerks used small oval seals which they wore around their necks or on finger rings. As with seals of lay men and women, The National Archives holds thousands of seals of clergymen from cardinals to humble parish priests.

The same is the case with perhaps the better-known and better-explored collection of seals of religious houses and of monks, nuns, canons, friars and other members of the religious orders who authenticated and validated written transactions throughout the Middle Ages.

Monastic seals, whether of individual houses or of individual people, are incredibly varied both in imagery and in the quality of the artistry employed. Unlike the seals of lay authorities and lay men and women, or of church institutions and churchmen, the survival of monastic seals is limited by the Dissolution of the Monasteries under Henry VIII in the 1530s and 1540s. Indeed, some of the best surviving examples come from the documents by which heads of monastic houses, abbots and abbesses, priors and prioresses, recognised Henry as Supreme Head of the Church of England in 1533/4, having been awarded the title of Defender of the Faith by Popes Leo X and Clement VII in 1523/4, or by which they surrendered their houses and properties to the king later in the 1530s.

SC 7/14/3: Confirmation to Henry VIII of the title Fidei Defensor, conferred upon him by Leo X and Clement VII 1523-1524; seal, obverse.

SC 7/14/3: Confirmation to Henry VIII of the title Fidei Defensor, conferred upon him by Leo X and Clement VII 1523-1524; seal and case, reverse.

An exquisite seal is that of John (Hammond), final abbot of the Benedictine house of Battle in Sussex, appended to the deed of the abbey's surrender to Henry VIII. The central figure on the obverse is John wearing his robes and mitre while holding a pastoral staff and book. He is flanked on one side by a saint with a palm branch above a shield with the quartered arms of France and England, a nod to its foundation by William the Conqueror after the Battle of Hastings and its subsequent royal patronage. On the other side is the figure of a bishop above another shield of arms. In a niche above the abbot is a depiction of the abbey's patron Saint Martin, the early Christian martyr, cutting his cloak for the beggar. This design had been used by John's predecessors for several centuries. On the reverse as a counterseal is an impression of the seal of the convent of Battle Abbey. This has a detailed and ornate engraving of the abbey church with the tall central tower and two smaller flanking towers. The legend around the edge reads '[SI]GILLVM CONVENTVS SANCTI MARTINI DE BELLO', ('Seal of the convent of Saint Martin of Battle').

E 322/16: Seal of Battle Abbey appended to the deed of surrender, 27 May 1538.

The Battle Abbey seal is a perfect blend of artistic flair to represent architectural realism, the patronage and history of the institution and its link to the crown, and the link of the abbot to his predecessors. It also reflects the genre itself, although the different monastic orders developed slightly different iconography over the centuries, and though the impression is late in the history of monastic sealing in England it belongs to a long-standing tradition.

E 322/188, seal of Cardinal College, Oxford, 15 January 1531.

E 322/241, seal of Thurgarton priory (Nottinghamshire), 14 June 1538.

Several monastic seals, those of the Benedictine abbeys at Athelney and Glastonbury in Somerset and Sherborne in Dorset, as well as the cathedral priories of Canterbury, Durham and Exeter, belong to the period before the Norman Conquest. These tend to show a stylised building; the final pre-Conquest seal, that of Edith, daughter of King Edgar (958/9-975) and half-sister of Edward the Martyr (975-978) and Æthelred the Unraed (978-1016), nun of Wilton (Wiltshire), shows, rather, the veiled figure of a woman in fine robes carrying a book. The legend reads 'Sigil Eadgyðe Re[ga]l[is] [Ad]elphe', ('The seal of Edith, the royal sister'). Remarkably, the community of nuns at Wilton held Edith in such reverence that they continued to use her seal until their dissolution in 1536 (though the surviving impression is at the British Library as Harley Charter 45 A 36).

After the Conquest, seals of monasteries generally used an image of the abbey building, and were therefore sometimes circular in shape, or of a central figure of an abbot within some kind of arched niche beneath a canopy and surrounded by symbols relevant to the patronage or history of the house. As many houses were dedicated to the Virgin Mary, particularly Cistercian monasteries, the central figure of a crowned, enthroned woman usually bearing a child was popular, though, of course, the central figure would change to whichever saint was the patron. Equally widespread were images of all three Persons of the Holy Trinity.

Perhaps the ultimate expression of the fusion of the power and mystery of faith and the beauty of art with the practical necessities of transacting legal and administrative business is the two-sided seal of the convent of Christ Church cathedral priory, Canterbury, one of the gems of the collection of The National Archives. Measuring just over nine centimetres in diameter, and being impressed in red wax, this seal, the matrix of which dates to c. 1230, represents a technological innovation. The obverse shows a richly detailed view of the West Front of the cathedral with a large double front door topped with a tympanum containing a bust of Christ. There are three towers, a large central tower flanked by two side towers attached to transepts. The steep roof has a clerestory below it of pointed arches. The transept towers both have a deep opening into which the heads, respectively, of Saints Alphega and Dunstan are inserted. The figure of an angel hangs down from the clouds above the central tower, shining Heavenly favour upon the convent. In front of the cathedral is the town wall with battlements and towers, encircling and protecting the community. The legend reads 'SIGILLVM ECCLESIE XPI [CAN]TUARIE PRIME SEDIS BRITANN[IE]', ('Seal of Christ's Church Canterbury, the Principal See of Britain').

On the reverse is a scene of the martyrdom of St Thomas Becket, former archbishop of Canterbury, the most meaningful and defining event in its history, which can be viewed through the great portal of the cathedral. The martyr kneels while his clerk Edmund Grim stands beside him with a cross. Two knights, one identifiable as Reginald fitz Urse, rush in and assassinate the archbishop. Above the portal, within three round arches, are two angels lifting Becket's soul to Heaven. A legend around the perimeter reads 'EST HVIC VITA MORI PRO QVA DVM VIXIT AMORI MORS ERAT ET MEMORI PER MORTEM VIVIT HONORI',

E 25/25: Oath of Supremacy, with seal of the convent of Christ Church Cathedral Priory, 12 December 1534, obverse.

E 25/25: Oath of Supremacy, with seal of the convent of Christ Church Cathedral Priory, 12 December 1534, reverse.

('This life is for death for which, while he lived, death became love and memory, for through death honour shall live'). The genius of the design is that the two-plated matrix works to impress images through as well as into the wax and required considerable skill to operate.

The seal of Christ Church cathedral priory is one of the ultimate expressions of the seal-maker's craft in the Middle Ages. It is a perfect marriage of art, ideas and technical skill with raw materials. To finish this book, we are now going to look briefly at some of those materials critical to the manufacture and use of seals throughout history.

CHAPTER 4

MATERIALS

Seals are artistic masterpieces rich in meaning and windows into the pre-modern world. However, they are also material objects that have passed down to us in various states of decay and disrepair. Their materiality – physical and chemical make-up – can tell us things a visual examination cannot. In this concluding chapter, we will take a brief look at how seals are composed, at how this changes over time and some of the various methods of attachment to the parent documents. This reveals something of the ritual and practice of sealing in the past.

Throughout the medieval period, seal impressions were generally made in beeswax (though the Papacy tended to use lead for its equivalent bulls). Neither England and its dominions nor Scotland could produce wax in sufficient quantity to meet the demand that the explosion of written culture created from the twelfth century onwards. Much of the wax that was imported into England came from eastern Europe and the Baltic, traded by merchants of the German Hanse, though some came from Africa with French and Spanish traders. Accounts of the English royal administration, surviving customs accounts and inventories of merchants' property demonstrate the range and varieties of wax on sale, whether this was in its natural, unprepared state or dyed, bulked out and specifically sold for sealing.

Beeswax was seen as an ideal substance for making seals as it becomes pliable and workable at 32C, so below human body temperature. Melting wax also permitted colorants (such as natural dyes) to be added with relative ease. This meant that wax could be heated to the right consistency either over fire, in hot water or even pressed between warmed hands, and then, like plasticine, moulded to receive the matrix and leave a crisp, permanent impression. Within the royal chancery, for example, it might be relatively straightforward to prepare wax in sufficient quantity, to the right colour and level of plasticity to accommodate the demands of the king and his royal administration. Once heated and softened, wax could be held and moulded in one hand and an impression made with the other – this produces a neat cup-shaped impression. Conversely, an individual might press wax into a matrix and leave a tell-tale finger imprint on the back (including in this example from the 'chancery' of Henry of Lancaster in 1301, the mark of fingernails made by the clerk involved in sealing). Such personal

E 26/1E Seal of Henry of Lancaster, 1301, obverse.

E 26/1E Seal of Henry of Lancaster, 1301, reverse.

impressions might have been left in certain contexts by the same individual – some towns or lords, for instance, may have delegated a particular person to do their sealing on important documents. Wax could also, as with the royal great seal, be sandwiched between two plates of a metal matrix and then released by the application of chalk or oil after being pressed or rolled (see Chapter 1).

In the first century or so after the Norman Conquest, many royal and aristocratic seal impressions were composed of natural, undyed wax. This looks creamy white in appearance now, which is sometimes the consequence of bleaching or the addition of chalk or alum. Wax could be consolidated with a variety of fillers, such as sand, hair, wool fibres or turpentine and balsam (or other kinds of coniferous plant resin), the latter of which could harden the wax and ensure it lasted longer. As a general rule, the use of natural wax for the rest of the medieval period was reserved for records deemed either to have temporary value, such as writs ordering specific, immediate action to be taken, or for duplicate 'office copies' of documents of a more formal nature, of which the crown wanted record. This is probably because of both the visual effect of colour and the higher status imbued by using more expensive, exotic materials.

Colour is a matter of real intrigue and importance in discussing medieval seals. For much of the Middle Ages, many royal charters and letters patent granting perpetual privileges, gifts, awards or commissioning officeholders, were authenticated with the Great Seal impressed in green wax. Green wax could be made in a number of ways. The most common natural mineral pigment for making it is malachite, which like other green minerals has a copper base. It could be ground down into a powder and then cooked with melted beeswax to create different shades of green. An alternative was verdigris, an artificial compound made from the chemical reaction of copper with organic acid vapours from things like vinegar or curdled milk, even urine, in a closed vessel. Verdigris has ancient origins and was not expensive to manufacture. Variations in the cooking time of wax with such copper-based pigments would lead to lighter or darker shades – the longer the cook (perhaps days), the darker the shade. A final method of manufacture was the melting of natural wax in a copper vessel like a kettle, which, as it oxidised in air, turned green. Similarly, the length of cooking time and exposure to oxygen might affect the shade of green produced. This would be a quick and relatively simple way of producing green, and we find many green seals throughout the surviving corpus, suggesting it was the easiest (and probably cheapest) colour to produce. It also suggests that having your seal dyed was a marker perhaps of some status or sophistication, or that you had access to resources beyond your usual means. The range of tones among surviving green seals can also be put down to the effects of ageing on different materials. Indeed, many seals which now appear brown may well have originally been green in hue as they too have copper-based pigmentation. Having said that, the brownish pigment kettle-brown was also employed during the Middle Ages and could produce seals genuinely brown in colour.

Copper and beeswax being heated together in a vessel.

Probably the most visually appealing and impressive seals are those coloured red. Seal owners from kings, the royal administration and aristocrats to wealthy merchants and townsmen used red wax for sealing documents. The early fourteenth-century accounts of the earls of Lancaster, kinsmen of the king, show that they bought large quantities of wax, the bright red pigment vermilion and turpentine for sealing documents across their broad estates in northwest England, the East and West Midlands and the Welsh Marches. Nevertheless, as the Middle Ages progressed, the colour became increasingly ubiquitous

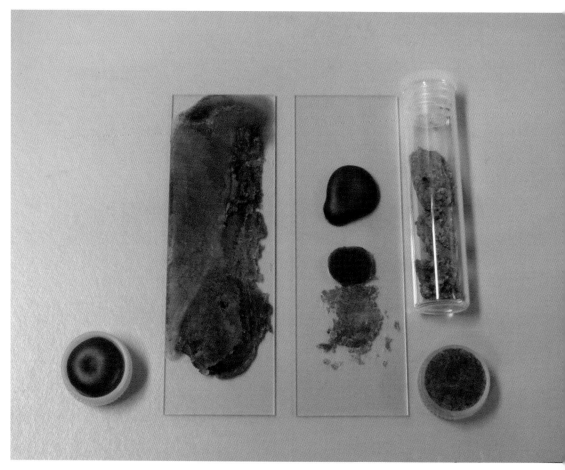

Modern experimentation with green pigmentation.

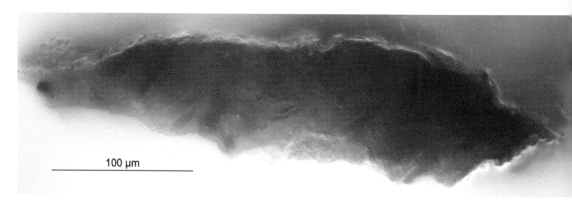

Cross-section of a 'brown' seal (E 26/1K), 1301.

and within government it became the default colour for the privy and signet seals. Red seals appear to have been more prestigious given the expense of the materials involved in making them: the most popular pigment was mercury sulphide, which is the chemical colorant used to produce vermilion by grinding and heating the mineral cinnabar. Red lead, produced by heating lead white to an orangey hue, was a cheaper alternative and could be manufactured in England and other parts of Europe where lead was mined. As with green wax, minor variations in quantities and purity of pigment involved, mixing and heating could create different tones, and also different levels of colour degradation over time. Researchers will regularly come across light pinkish seals and dark red examples.

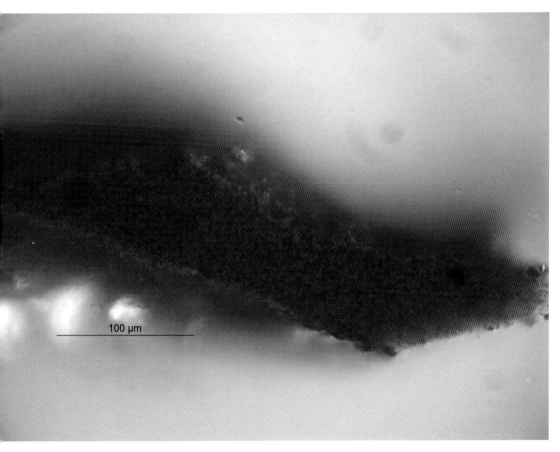

Cross-section of the pigmentation in the seal of the Empress Matilda (DL 10/17), 1141x1142.

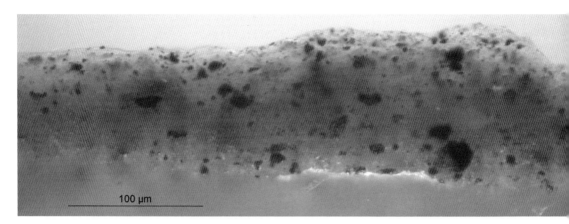

Cross-section of the pigmentation in the seal of Henry of Lancaster (E 26/1E), 1301.

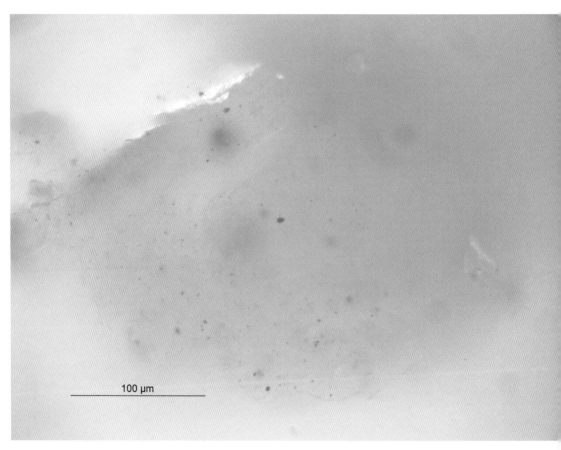

Cross-section of the pigmentation of the seal of Christ Church Cathedral, Canterbury (E 25/25), 1534.

The visual appeal of the red seal in hand – and its longer-term preservation – could be enhanced, too, by the application of varnish or paint. The addition of varnish, paint and, to a greater extent, resin served to harden the wax. Over time, they could make it more brittle too, and many, many seals survive as fragments. Basic handling of seals, even with care, can leave tiny granules or larger chips behind. Medieval seal-makers recognised the problem of poorer quality materials. For some personal seals from the later Middle Ages we find straw applied in a circle around the impression, which stands out particularly on red seals. This attempted to strengthen the impression. Another method developed, at least in its infancy, around this time was the use of the so-called 'wafer'; this was a mixture of flour and water in a paste applied over the wax to prevent still warm and sticky wax adhering to the parchment or paper when the document was folded for dispatch.

'Painted' seals (DL 25/616), c. 1200.

Wafer technology improved over time so that it was in regular use, and produced better quality impressions on the face of documents, particularly during the nineteenth and twentieth centuries. A wafer Great Seal also came into use at this time. The wafer worked alongside the major early modern innovation in sealing material; from the sixteenth century, exploration and better access to Asian markets promoted the use of shellac as a replacement for wax. Shellac is the resinous secretion of the insect *Tachardia lacca*, which is native to Southeast Asia. Though more brittle than sealing wax and plasticky in look and feel, once melted it works well for closing documents and is versatile.

Time and tide, of course, wait for no man and when, in 2001, a new Great Seal was commissioned for Elizabeth II, it was impressed into a synthetic compound and has been ever since.

One thing to remember with seals is that they do not exist simply as objects in their own right, beautiful though many are. They relate closely to the text of the document to which they are attached, and clauses in the document often make specific reference to the seal, which helps us identify the owner or the circumstances under which the seal (or seals) was attached. More than the text, however, the method of attachment of the seal to its document can also tell us important things. Documents deemed to be of the very highest importance and status – treaties, diplomatic correspondence with foreign powers and dignitaries, charters and letters patent – could be attached to the document using silk cords or laces, often multi-coloured with dyestuffs and multiple strands delicately and skilfully woven together. At this level, the visual effect and display of status was as important as the practical appending to the document.

For documents of perhaps less political and diplomatic importance, or of a more ephemeral nature like written instructions to officials, a tag made from a cut strip of parchment would be affixed to the wax. Within government, simple writs issuing such instructions might only be sealed with a dab of white wax pressed into part of the Great Seal matrix and so sealed 'with the foot of the seal' hanging from a tongue cut about two thirds of the way through the bottom of the parchment on which the text was written. It is also not uncommon to find parchment tags with writing on them as the officials in government, the church, or in private households re-used old or draft documents to save money.

Close up of the attachment of seal cords to DL 10/18, 1141.

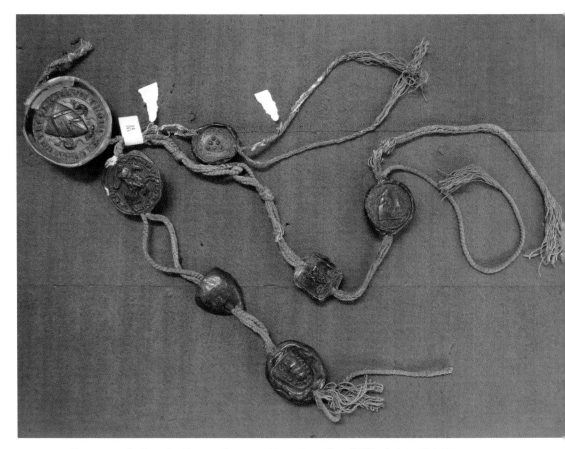

Laces attached to the Barons Letter to Pope Boniface VIII of 1301, E 26/1.

Whether cords or tags, the method of attachment was usually squeezed between the cakes of wax once softened and before the impression was made by the matrix. That way they would permanently form a single whole. With parchment tags, sometimes a slit would be made down the middle and a knot formed in order to make a surface from which softened wax could not easily slide off.

There could, however, be more than one way to attach the seal and its tag or cords to the physical document. For parchment tags, a simple slit might be made in the plica – the fold at the foot of the document – and the tag threaded through. Several holes would be needed for cords or laces to be threaded through and then knots tied in the cords to ensure they could not slip back out. Either way, simple but effective techniques were used to secure a seal to its document. After all, the validity of the text depended on the validation and authentication of the seal.

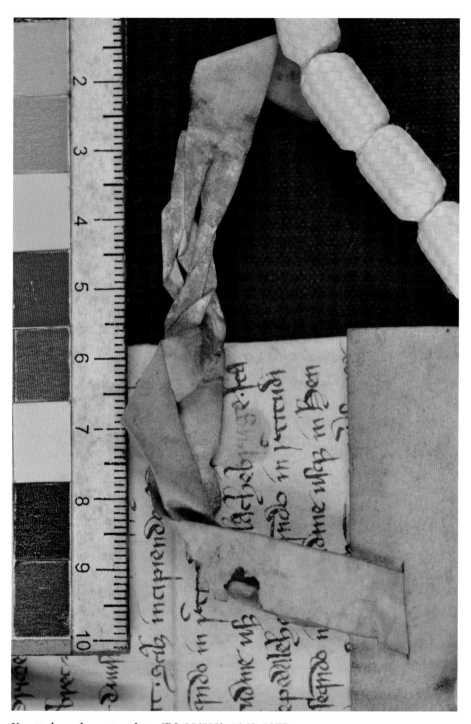

Knotted parchment seal tag (DL 25/592), 1260x1272.

Fragment of parchment now detached from the Barons' Letter to Pope Boniface VIII (E 26/1, cord Z), 1301.

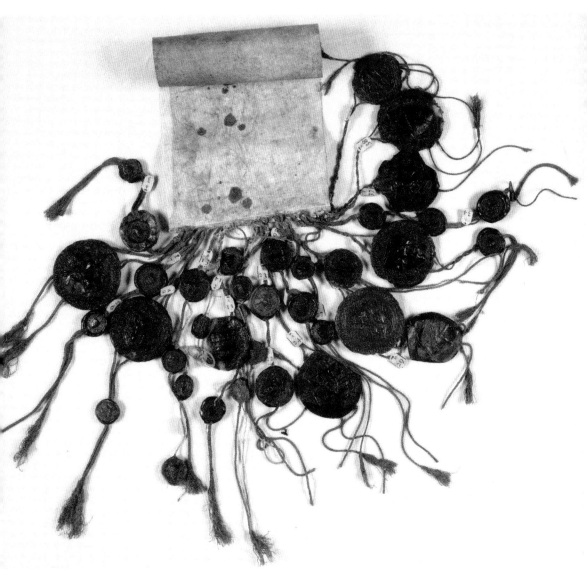

Barons' Letter to Pope Boniface VIII (E 26/1), 1301, before conservation.

BIBLIOGRAPHY

Adams, N., Cherry, J. and Robinson, J. (eds), *Good Impressions: Image and Authority in Medieval Seals* (London, 2008)

Birch, W. de Gray, *Catalogue of Seals in the Department of Manuscripts in the British Museum*, 6 vols (London, 1887-1900)

Cherry, J., Berenbeim J. and de Beer, L., (eds), *Seals and Status: The Power of Objects* (London: British Museum Research Publication 213, 2018)

Clanchy, M.T., *From Memory to Written Record: England 1066-1307* (Oxford, 1993)

Ellis, R.H., (ed), *Catalogue of Seals in the Public Record Office* (London, 1978-86), 3 volumes: I-II *Personal Seals*; III: *Monastic Seals*

Harvey, P.D.A. and McGuinness, A., *A Guide to British Medieval Seals* (London, 1996)

Jenkinson, H.C., (ed), *Guide to Seals in the Public Record Office* (2nd edition: London, 1968)

McEwan, J.A., *Seals in Medieval London, 1050-1300. A Catalogue* (London Record Society Extra Series 1, 2016)

McEwan, J.A. and New, E., *Seliau yn eu Cyd-destun: Cymru a'r Mers yn yr Oesoedd Canol/Seals in Context: Medieval Wales and the Welsh Marches* (Aberystwyth, 2012)

Schofield, P., (ed), *Seals and the Context in the Middle Ages* (Oxford, 2015)

Whatley, L.J., (ed), *A Companion to Seals in the Middle Ages* (Leiden, 2019)

Wyon, A.B. and Wyon, A., *The Great Seals of England: from the earliest period to the present time, arranged and illustrated with descriptive and historical notes* (London, 1887)